GREEN'S NOT YOUR BEST COLOR

Mieka Phillips

being an original girl in a plastic world

an imprint of
Standard Publishing
www.rfgbooks.com

This book is dedicated to my family, who exhibit the patience of Job and the love of Christ. But above all, this book is for every young lady that God has woven and will weave into the tapestry of my life. Thank you for letting me walk with you through this crazy world! Remember, you are not alone!

. . . .

Green's Not Your Best Color

© 2006 Mieka Phillips.

Published by Standard Publishing, Cincinnati, Ohio. A division of Standex International Corporation. All rights reserved. No part of this book may be reproduced in any form, except for brief quotations in reviews, without the written permission of the publisher. refuge™ is a trademark of Standard Publishing. Printed in China. Editor: Dale Reeves. Project editor: Laura Derico. Content editor: Jennifer Grosser. Cover and interior design: Brand Navigation.

All Scripture quotations, unless otherwise indicated, are taken from the Holy Bible, *New Living Translation,* copyright © 1996. Used by permission of Tyndale House Publishers, Inc., Wheaton, Illinois 60189. All rights reserved. Those marked *The Message* are taken from *The Message,* copyright © 1993, 1994, 1995, 1996, 2000, 2001, 2002. Used by permission of NavPress Publishing Group. Those marked NIV are taken from the HOLY BIBLE, NEW INTERNATIONAL VERSION®. NIV®. Copyright © 1973, 1978, 1984 by International Bible Society. Used by permission of Zondervan. All rights reserved.

ISBN 0-7847-1842-3

12 11 10 09 08 07 06   9 8 7 6 5 4 3 2 1

Library of Congress Cataloging-in-Publication Data

Phillips, Mieka, 1972-
  Green's not your best color / Mieka Phillips.
    p. cm.
  ISBN 0-7847-1842-3 (casebound)
  1. Teenage girls--Religious life. 2. Christian life--Biblical teaching. I. Title.

BV4551.3.P45 2006
248.8'33--dc22

2005026763

CONTENTS

INTRODUCTION

OK, look, plastic is not a bad thing. Some of my way cool childhood memories involve plastic; I remember my yellow Garfield™ lunch box, my Slinky® spring toy, my Hula-Hoop® plastic hoop, my obscene number of Strawberry Shortcake™ dolls, and my Shrinky Dinks® toy kit. I killed many an afternoon with these plastic playmates! I also have fun memories of dressing up my cat and pushing it down the street in my plastic shopping cart. And I'll never forget my all-time favorite pastime—crawling into displays at the department stores and posing with the plastic mannequins! I was a pro!

But, you know, we're not made from plastic, and God never intended for us to act like we are. Yet how often do we cover up our feelings just to keep someone from seeing our vulnerability? Or how many times do we bite our tongues and not say what we really think, afraid of sounding too different or weird? We nod and blink our way through life with a painted-on face, hoping just to blend in.

God desires more for us. He wants us to take off the masks . . . to be thinking, feeling, passionate and even vulnerable people. It's a process that takes a long time, particularly in the fake world we live in. Think about it, people don't even outgrow their love for plastic as adults—slide those credit cards!

I wrote **Green's Not Your Best Color** to encourage you to be an original in this plastic world. The material in this book is based on specific Scriptures and on my personal experiences from living on this roller coaster we call life! Not too far removed from being a teenage girl myself, I experienced firsthand most of the junk that gets thrown at you. I'm still right there with you in spirit. I now teach high school and interact every day with young women and the crazy problems that you face. And to be honest, I still read some of the very things I wrote and think, *Man, I've gotta work on that!*

These studies or devotionals can be used in a personal quiet time, a Sunday school class, or as part of a small group Bible study. The **Anything But Plastic** study questions that are included with each reading can be answered in one sitting or reflected on throughout the week. Take however much time you need to meditate on the Scripture and the topic, and to link the concepts discussed in the reading to your own life.

The last part of each study is entitled **Beyond Plastic**. This section presents a challenge for you: maybe to think more about a particular issue, or to interact with people around you, or to spend some more time with God.

Part of your journey in your daily walk as a Christian is to move away from the cold, unfeeling plastic ways of the world toward a warm and active walk that is very much alive in Christ. What a journey—from plastic to originality! Step out from behind those mannequins, melt down that frozen smile and get real!

We will not compare ourselves with each other. . . .
We have far more interesting things to do with our lives.
Each of us is an original.

Galatians 5:26 (The Message)

THAT REALLY MAKES ME MAD!

*The Lord is slow to anger and rich in unfailing love,
forgiving every kind of sin and rebellion.*

Numbers 14:18

One of my responsibilities as a school-teacher is to maintain communication with my students' parents, particularly in the case of a student who is doing poorly and may even be in danger of failing. Perhaps your parents have received a phone call from one of your teachers before.

At the end of one grading period, I made a series of phone calls. Even though it is technically a part of my job, it is very hard to find time to do it, so I felt quite smug in taking extra time to be concerned for my students in my efforts to save the world! Up until my fourth phone call, I received very positive feedback from all of the parents to whom I had spoken. Yeah for me! Pats on my back! My elation quickly faded, however, when I hung up the receiver from the

next phone call, feeling stung as if I had been slapped across the face. The mother that I had just spoken to had spent our conversation accusing *me* for her son's failing grade!

She told me, "You know, he is just like that. If you talk to his teachers, they'll tell you that this lack of effort and the failing grades are a pattern with him. I'm trying to get him in for counseling because I don't know what's wrong with him. He won't do anything at home. You teachers are going to have to talk to him. Find out why he's acting like this. You'll have to make him do it, because I can't."

I could hardly believe my ears—this kid doesn't even belong to me. I didn't give birth to him! But I'm being asked to take the blame for his failure in my

French class! I spent the rest of the afternoon feeling bitter—angry that I had even wasted my time trying to talk to this student's mother. And then it hit me. Didn't Christ do the very thing for me that I resented doing for my student? When I was a sinner, when I was the one *not* doing the work, not carrying my load—didn't Christ take the blame for me? He died on the cross for my mistakes, my laziness, my insecurities and my shame. He could just as easily have said, "She's not my problem. I can't figure her out. Let someone else counsel her. Someone else will have to make her straighten up. I can't do it!"

But God did not give up on me. That afternoon, this reminder of God's faithfulness humbled me. I realized that instead of praying for this guy, his situation and the insight for his mother to know how to handle him, I got my feathers ruffled and only thought about how I felt on my end of the deal. The Holy Spirit reminded me that Christ's example should motivate me not to give up on my student. He may still fail my class; but I will help him carry his cross.

Thank goodness God does not give up on you and me. I am sure there are times that he would like to. But I am learning that he does not reject me when I frustrate him; not only does he not reject me, but he continues to love me with an unconditional love, rather than acting in anger and bitterness toward me. Aren't you glad that God allows us to be his "problems"?

Anything But Plastic

. . . .

1. Is anger a problem for you? Has someone else's anger had some sort of effect on your life? If so, where and when do these problems tend to rear their ugly heads?

2. Read Proverbs 15:1. What does this verse say that harsh words do?

    Can you recall a specific situation when you calmed someone's anger? Or did someone do this for you? Explain.

3. Read Ephesians 4:26. In this passage, Paul encourages you to deal with unrighteous anger right away. Typically, how are you about harboring bitterness or holding a grudge?

    Do you storm off in heated situations and wait for the other person to chase you down and apologize first, or do you attempt to fix the problem and help heal the rift?

4. Read 1 Timothy 2:8. What does Paul say prayer should be without?

Have you ever attempted to pray when you were upset with someone? What was your prayer like as a result of your anger? Do you feel that your time spent with God while you were angry was meaningful? Was your prayer effective?

5. In 1 Samuel 25, a man named Nabal insults David and David gets so angry, he wants to kill him and his whole family. Read 1 Samuel 25:23-35 to find out what Nabal's wife, Abigail, did. What kinds of things did she say to calm David's anger? What was the result?

Read on through verse 42. What blessing did David see by not acting out in anger?

Beyond Plastic . . . .

The battle of anger can be won as you allow the Holy Spirit to control your life. He longs to give you victory in this area as you yield to him. If this is what you truly desire, I encourage you to voice your concerns to God in prayer.

ANYTIME NOW, GOD

*The Lord will work out his plans for my life—for your faithful love,
O Lord, endures forever. Don't abandon me, for you made me.*

Psalm 138:8

My mother is an avid gardener. She can make *anything* grow. She inherited this ability to cultivate things from her father. I don't remember much about my grandfather. I was too little. But my mom can remember everything about him. She remembers waking up in the morning to the sound of my Papa whistling as he tended the garden behind her house; she hung out with him while he tinkered with the car. My mom says that she never heard an unkind word from Papa's mouth. I figure that subconsciously my mom gardens because it makes her feel close to him, since he passed away many years ago. I think she also gardens for stress relief and perhaps to feel a nearness to God as she works in his creation.

I, on the other hand, am a different piece of work altogether! I have nothing that even remotely resembles a green thumb. All I can cultivate is mold on a loaf of bread. My mom assures me that I *could* master the skill of gardening, since I finally grasped the cooking thing. But until I actually have the time to commit to gardening, I would rather just enjoy her talent.

One summer, as a result of her hard work, the traffic flow increased quite a bit on my parents' back deck! At almost any time of day, you could stand at the kitchen window, and right before your eyes, the plants became the hottest hangout for neighborhood butterflies.

After much observation, I began to wonder if God kept sending these butterflies to teach me some kind of lesson. Each butterfly had a different color and size: black-and-orange monarchs, yellow-and-black ones, solid yellow, solid orange and even several with beautiful sky blue painted across their wings. I encountered them in the garden, on the rearview mirror of my car, and one day one flew in front of me while I waited at a traffic light.

There had to be a point in there somewhere, so after slipping into nature channel mode, I looked the word *butterfly* up in a book we have called *Character Sketches*. I learned some interesting things about these fascinating creatures. The most impressive thing was that a butterfly passes through four distinct phases of life. It begins as an egg and then develops into a larva or a caterpillar. Then during the larva stage, it sheds its skin approximately four times to allow room for growth. Once the caterpillar matures, it encases itself inside a cocoon and enters into what is known as a pupa stage. Finally it exits the cocoon as a magnificent butterfly.

After phase four, upon entering the big world from the cocoon, the butterfly's wings are undeveloped. But within minutes the muscle system works, forcing fluid to the wings, making them grow. With exposure to the air, the butterfly's body firms up and becomes capable of flying. But it takes great struggles and hard work for the butterfly to reach maturity—some skin-shedding, a lot of spinning and a lot of flapping. Each of these four stages is a necessary part of becoming a butterfly.

So what conclusions did I draw from this butterfly escapade? My friends, I think you and I are a lot like butterflies. I believe that we are all in a hurry to get to that final phase—to burst onto the world's stage as beautiful creatures worth being noticed. I believe that in our rush, we are all too often lazy and impatient. We cut corners in the phases of growth that we've got to go through. I know *I'm* guilty of this!

I wonder which stage of my butterfly life I'm in at present? I figure I'm past the egg phase. Maybe I'm in the four-time-skin-shedding phase, itching and scratching as God methodically peels away layers of fear, insecurity and fakeness. And since God develops his children gradually, this could take years! Or maybe I'm encased in my silken cocoon, chillin' in pupa-land. There's a chance I have emerged already, but I'm just waiting for the juices to flow so I can unfold my beautiful wings and fly in the maturity of Christ.

My point is, life is a series of phases. You and I do not enter this world in a state of perfection. We are not born with some great identity. I am clueless as to how I fit into the growth process, but I'm going to guess that I look more like a worm than a butterfly. I do know this about myself. I am *so* impatient.

But what if I mess things up? Will God be disappointed in me? Will he neglect his project? I hope not. I'd hate for him to abandon me due to my selfishness and impatience. After all, I've really got it easy. Abraham waited almost one hundred years to be a father and then had a chart-topping number of children. Job endured a tremendous amount of suffering in order to cross over to the peace and growth on the other side of the pain.

Where are you today? Are you an egg? a larva? Are you hanging in the pupa phase? Wherever it is, be certain of this—if it concerns you, the Lord will accomplish it. Is it really worth the rush to get there? I know, sometimes we think it is. I don't know about you, but I want to emerge from life's phases and tests of patience as something that's worth looking at. I want to be like a butterfly, so that when others look at me they will understand that God is a patient God who does not forsake the works of his hands.

Ask God to help you endure the phases of growth he has for you. Allow him to create a butterfly out of you. Unlike me, he can grow a lot more than mold!

Anything But Plastic

1. There are many aspects of any Christian's character and attitude that God may not be finished working on yet. Despite your efforts to work on your weaknesses and to give them to God in prayer, you will still struggle with things—it's human nature. What are some things about your character that you know are still in that skin-shedding phase?

2. What are some things that you want to accomplish or become in your life? List several.

3. Read the following verses and answer the questions.

   Luke 8:15. What produces a good harvest?

   Hebrews 6:12. Who does the writer tell us to be like?

   James 1:4. What does this verse say?

So, from these verses, what do you need to do or have in order to become what God made you to be?

4. As a teenager, you sometimes see other girls who have every appearance of being a perfect "butterfly." They seem talented, beautiful and smart on the outside—and they may be all of those things . . . but they might not. Read Matthew 23:27. According to this verse, what is sometimes true about people or things that outwardly seem to have it all together?

How important is it to you that your inside appears as beautiful as your outside?

5. Read Ecclesiastes 3:11. According to this verse, with a right heart and a focus on Christ, when do you think that you will become beautiful?

Beyond Plastic

Be patient! God knows what he is doing with every one of his creations. In this crazy world, sometimes a little extra time in a cocoon as a pupa doesn't look half bad!

UGLY GRUDGES

Get rid of all bitterness, rage, anger, harsh words, and slander, as well as all types of malicious behavior.

Ephesians 4:31

This verse makes me think of my good friend, Meg Ryan. All right, Meg and I don't really know each other, but I've spent a lot of time with her and her chick flicks on my dateless Friday nights.

One of my all-time favorite Meg Ryan films is *French Kiss*. In this movie she plays "Kate," a schoolteacher who hastily decides to take a plane to Paris in order to search for her fiancé. He has been charmed by the powers of the city of love and has fallen for another girl. En route to France, Kate is unavoidably seated next to a French crook named Luc. Apparently not one another's type, the two opposites become a comic pair on a quest to help each other solve life's immediate problems. During their adventures through France, Kate confronts Luc about his negative attitude. She tells him that when he is old, she will find him all shriveled up, festering and rotting. "Fester, fester, fester; rot, rot, rot!" she proclaims, imitating his French accent with added grumpiness.

Although I laugh at this scene almost every time I watch this classic, I also feel a bitter sting. Unfortunately, there are times when I can see Luc's bad attitude reflected in my own life. How guilty am I of "festering and rotting"? I can be the world's worst case of someone festering and being slow to forgive . . . and not *quite* forget. Just call me "Queen Fester." I can pray about an issue and smooth things over, but on the inside, I often have great difficulty letting my anger and bitterness go.

Being free of this attitude should be so simple. God sent Christ to earth to endure grave circumstances and set the ultimate example for us. If anyone had reason to be bitter, Christ did. People pursued him, rejected him, mocked him and killed him—all of this despite his innocence. But God knows fully the earthly pain his Son endured. And since Christ, as a man, could stand strong despite the negativity around him, God thus gives us the command to put anger and bitterness aside and to forgive, tenderheartedly.

Of course, this command isn't so easy for humans to follow. If it were, then I don't think I would selfishly hold on to grudges from last week, last spring and even ten years ago. But humans are often hypersensitive and jealous. It is human nature to look at ourselves constantly in comparison to others. There will always be people who are better than we are, who get more attention than we do, who make us angry or seem to obtain things unfairly. There is no doubt about that! But the question is, how do we handle these human situations in which we do not always come out on top?

Festering and rotting are not particularly attractive qualities. God calls us to a much higher response than that. What attitude will people find in you today or next week, let alone when you are older? Will you be shriveled up in bitterness with an unforgiving heart, or will you allow God to renew your spirit and to help you approach each new situation with a refreshed attitude?

Anything But Plastic

1. Let's talk bitterness. Consider bitter food for a moment. What foods or smells do you think are bitter?

   How would you describe a person who is bitter? List some adjectives or phrases.

   Do your behavior and actions ever match this description of a bitter person—even just a little? How do you reflect bitterness in your life?

2. Read 1 Samuel 1:10. Hannah was sad because she wanted a child so much. What did she do?

   What are some things that have happened to cause bitterness in you? Have you been able to get over your bitterness? How?

3. Bitterness is almost always linked to sometime when you don't get what you want—and someone else does! Read James 4:1-3. Has bitter jealousy ever caused quarreling in your life? When? What did you do about it?

Think of a time when you asked God for something and you didn't get it. Did you get bitter about it? Think about your motives at the time. Do you think they were right or wrong? Why?

It can be really hard to get rid of bitter feelings. But read James 4:8. How do you think you need to draw closer to God?

3. Regardless of its place in your life, bitterness is not a very useful quality if you wish to resemble Christ in your attitude, your heart and your demeanor. Read Hebrews 12:15. What does this verse say to watch out for?

In some Bible versions the first sentence in this verse says that no one should miss the grace of God. In what ways might holding on to bitterness make you miss out on God's grace?

Beyond Plastic . . . .

After your proper grieving time, you should truly dump the bitterness! Festering and rotting don't make for a fun and attractive look. You don't want to be found in your old age shriveled up from holding grudges. God can help you forgive and forget the painful things and hurtful people in your life.

ENJOY THE RIDE

*Some nations boast of their [chariots and horses],
but we boast in the Lord our God.*

Psalm 20:7

We've all seen it. The setting is a four-way stop or a traffic light; the time is whenever other cars are around; and the person behind the wheel is a teenager. The light turns green, the engine revs and the car is off in a cloud of dust leaving only the screech of tires echoing through the air. It is one of the most exciting times in a teenager's life—the enrollment in driver's ed, testing for a license and, if you are really lucky, parents handing over the keys to the car. It doesn't seem to matter whether the car is new or old, yours or Mom and Dad's—having access to and driving a car are some of your longest-awaited moments ever!

I am not attempting to say that starting to drive should not be an exciting time in a teenager's life. Nor am I accusing every

teenager of driving in the manner that I described above. But I am bringing the object of the car itself and your manner of driving it into the light. Most of us begin wanting a car long before we can drive. Cars in themselves are great things, but how we use cars and how important they are to us are things we might need to analyze.

I have endured many frustrations concerning cars. I was never fortunate enough to have one during high school. In fact, I didn't have my first car until my last year in college—six years after I learned how to drive! I remember well the number of years that I had to depend on anyone and everyone with a car to take me where I needed to go. I walked many blisters onto my feet during college when I got tired of asking for rides. But when you have a car of your own, it's easy to take it for granted.

Surprisingly enough, the Bible speaks to us on this very subject. Well, OK, not exactly. Of course, there were no cars in biblical times, but there were "wheels"—chariots! I don't know that there were as many colors and designs to choose from, but it was definitely *the* mode of transportation for the rich and mighty. And even that many years ago some people put too much stock in their vehicles. Psalm 20 tells us that there were nations who boasted in their chariots, bragging about these symbols of their might and power.

I would hate for people to think I bragged more about my car or other material things and trusted more in those things than in my Lord. Cars are destructible and so are we. Just like everything else, cars are a gift from God. If you are lucky enough to have a car, consider yourself truly blessed.

However, if you consider yourself the unlucky owner of a pair of feet instead of a set of wheels, you are not alone. I know what this is like. I have walked—literally—in your shoes. But being carless is not totally bad—you don't owe money for gas, insurance or car payments, and you are not responsible in the same way for someone else's safety. You do not have a car to distract you from a genuine trust in Christ. Regardless of whether you own a car or not, put your confidence in him. Some boast in chariots. You can brag about your God rather than a piece of metal.

Anything But Plastic

1. Maybe you have a car, or maybe you don't. Maybe having your own car isn't even going to happen anytime soon! How do you feel about your car status?

2. It is only natural to be excited about your car. After all, it is typically one of your first big items of responsibility or status. However, there are lots of people who don't realize the responsibility that comes with having a car. Do you know people who drive recklessly and do stupid things with their cars? What do you think about that?

   Do you know someone who has been seriously hurt, or worse, in a car wreck? What effects did the accident have?

3. What do you think of when you hear the word *inheritance*? What things have you been given by your parents, grandparents, etc. that you didn't ask for or maybe don't deserve?

   Read 1 Peter 1:3-6. Despite the value of material things, what is your only inheritance that will last?

4. Read 2 Corinthians 10:13. What did Paul say they would not brag about?

Read verses 17 and 18. What should we boast about? Why do you think Paul says this?

5. Read Matthew 6:19-21. What are you supposed to store up for yourself? What are some of the earthly things you collect or store up? What does verse 19 say could happen to these things?

How do you think you can work on storing up treasures in Heaven?

Beyond Plastic . . . .

You won't be taking the things you listed above with you when you leave this earth. No, not even that cool car. So ask God to show you a better perspective on your worldly toys and to show you what treasures of Heaven you can be working for!

THE BIG PICTURE

Without wavering, let us hold tightly to the hope we say we have. . . . Do not throw away this confident trust in the Lord, no matter what happens. Remember the great reward it brings you! Patient endurance is what you need now, so you will continue to do God's will.

Hebrews 10:23, 35, 36

Christmas season always rolls in sooner than expected and rushes out just as quickly. December days go by in a blur now, yet it seems like yesterday that I was a child waiting with impatience, thinking that Christmas would never come.

There are still some things like Christmas that I anxiously await with that childlike anticipation: answers to prayers that I've prayed forever, good things to happen to my family and a change in career. I guess in some ways I am really no different now from when I was a child.

Picture the Christmas tradition of Advent calendars. I remember how my sister and I took turns opening the calendar doors. We would alternate days, taking the secret prize that lay behind each door. Behind each piece of chocolate, a portion of a larger picture always awaited. As a child of course the candy was the best part, but it was fun to see the hidden picture as well. It was not until the December 25th door was opened that my sister and I were able to see the entire Advent picture.

I have discovered lately that my life feels a great deal like the inner workings of an Advent calendar. I feel as if on some days, God opens a little door for me and allows me to get a small glimpse of the secret mystery that hides behind it. But then a setback occurs. Rather than leave the preceding doors open so I can view the picture as it unfolds, God in his perfect timing quietly shuts the door and then pops another one open.

Of course, God's answers to my prayers don't come packaged in a twenty-five-day revelation. Wouldn't I be ecstatic if they did? Answers to prayer and "open windows" to God's plan sometimes come as readily as we ask for them, but sometimes a window may take a month to open. Sometimes they take even longer to be revealed. In my impatient frustration, I just want to rip the whole cover off of the Advent calendar of my life and catch sight of the big picture. Maybe I could better await the unknown things of the future if I just knew *when* the answers would come.

On the other hand, I'm beginning to realize that in my impatience, I've put God into the small boxes of my faith, just like the squares on an Advent calendar. I can only picture him working in one small window of my life, since that is all I get to see at one time. My small faith has minimized just how *huge* my God is and all he can do for a faithful heart!

At this very moment, God moves to and fro behind the individual windows of my life. He is not confined to these small windows as opportunities, and he doesn't want my faith to focus only on one small window at a time either. I must believe in a big God who has complete control over the big picture of my life. I know—easier said than done! But after all, God does call us to a childlike faith. Perhaps rather than moping about the unknown, I should search each open door of my life as an eager child opens each day on an Advent calendar. The great thing about the child is that he knows beyond a shadow of a doubt that a great surprise is always there waiting. The child never worries that the treat will come up missing. The secret is simply being patient enough to get the prize.

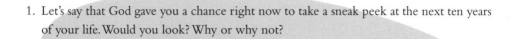

Anything But Plastic

1. Let's say that God gave you a chance right now to take a sneak peek at the next ten years of your life. Would you look? Why or why not?

   What would you like your life to look like ten years from now if you could choose? What do you want to achieve?

2. Talk about faith is often clichéd. When people refer to faith or faith in God, they use expressions such as:

   "You can do it! I have faith in you!"
   "God is so faithful!"
   "We must have faith in God."
   "All it takes is a little faith!"

   These all sound good, but what does it really mean to *be* faithful? What do you think the word *faithful* means?

   Now look the word up and give a dictionary definition.

   Finally, read Hebrews 11:1. According to this verse, what is faith?

3. Read each of the following Scriptures and give a one- or two-word description of God.

Deuteronomy 7:9:

2 Thessalonians 3:3:

1 John 1:9:

4. In Matthew 25:14-30, Jesus tells a story about a man who went on a trip and gave his servants money to invest for him. Read verses 19-23. What did the two who were called "good and faithful" do to receive this praise?

Read verses 24-30. What happened to the third servant? Why?

What do you think verse 29 means in regard to serving Christ?

Have you been unfaithful with what God has given you? List the areas where you think you lack faithful action.

Beyond Plastic . . . .

Let's get busy together in being faithful servants. I don't want to take away God's pleasure in blessing us with the best things and his perfect timing. After all, he knows the big picture!

SOMEONE'S WATCHING

You may not know this, but pretty much all around Texas there is an obsession with dance. Kids around here would give their right arm to be on the school dance team. Drill team contests last all weekend long and late into the night, just to declare a winner in a specific dance category or in the overall high school division.

I've been a full-fledged part of this crazy world since I was a little girl. In elementary school, when grown-ups asked me the inevitable what-do-you-want-to-be-when-you-grow-up question, I would bypass the expected doctor, lawyer and mommy replies and say without hesitation, "I want to be a Highstepper." *Highsteppers* is the name of my high school drill team. They've always

been good because for twenty-five years, they have operated under a high standard of excellence and self-motivation. The director set the bar high and expected much out of us.

I took these same standards away from high school and into my life with me. As a result, God mixed these values, my passion for dance and my love for kids, together in order to help shape my future. For the first six years of my career, I actually went back to help teach the Highsteppers. In this job, I tried to pour these standards of excellence back into my students.

So now these girls, in addition to all of my French students, make up *my* great crowd of witnesses! Although it freaks me out a bit at times, I've got to say that I have grown to like my accountability to this gang!

You know how high school is. Sometimes putting an adult in that environment is like throwing a fish in a shark tank. If the students don't like one of their teachers, they'll eat her for lunch! But God has placed me with these young men and women for a purpose. I love them! (Well, most days I do!) I guess I am young enough that they still trust me for advice and *sometimes* if I'm living right, they even think I'm kind of cool! Because of my relationship with them, I often depend on them to hold me accountable for my actions. Sometimes I think to myself, *What would kids think if they heard me say that or if they saw me do that?*

Of course, there are times when I wish I didn't live in a fishbowl. When you've taught hundreds and hundreds of kids, there's always that chance that anywhere you go you might run into one or five of them—eyes watching, ears listening and mouths ready to spread word of any mistake. But however nice my privacy might be, having this crowd around always helps me keep my walk straight.

Whether my students know it or not, their daily presence in my life keeps me accountable. I'm more aware of my thoughts, my actions and the words that roll off of my tongue. The Holy Spirit may use me to minister to teenagers, but this crowd of witnesses, hot on my heels and so quick to correct, helps me to run ahead—to stay just in front of them as a role model, trying to abstain from things that would cause them to stumble or keep them from growing in Christ. Even if they are not Christians, they watch, they listen, and they are not afraid to ask questions, put me on the spot or stick me to the wall!

Is there someone in your life who you look up to? Whose crowd are you a part of? Remember, that person is not perfect and has bad days too. But as a part of that crowd, you *should* expect much out of them! Don't be afraid to expect a lot from yourself as well. God has surrounded *you* with a crowd of witnesses. Keep limber, stay active and fit for the race because that crowd will keep you on your toes. You never know where God is using you— maybe even to minister to someone older than you. Pretty cool, huh?

Anything But Plastic

1. Look at Hebrews 12:1, 2 again. Below, write anything from the verse that jumps out at you and how you think it applies to your life at this time.

Whose crowd of witnesses are you in? Whom has God put in your life that you watch, expecting to see godly behavior? What is it that you watch in this "runner" for Christ? What do you learn from them?

2. Who is in your crowd? In other words, to whom are *you* accountable?

As you run, what tends to slow you down and hinder your race? What path do you think God has you on at this time in your life?

3. You may not be aware that you are surrounded by a crowd of witnesses. But remember, just because you can't see them, it doesn't mean they aren't there!

Look up the following words in the dictionary and briefly define them.

integrity:

character:

personality:

4. Are there some things in your life that you are hiding from your witnesses? In what areas of your life is your character not consistent with your personality? For example, are you sweet and funny with your teachers and friends, but obnoxious at home? Be honest with yourself. Where in your life are you inconsistent?

Beyond Plastic

I challenge you to memorize Hebrews 12:1, 2. For me, these verses have been a source of encouragement and strength time after time as I make decisions for my life and for the benefit of my crowd!

WHO'S CALLING THE SHOTS?

Take delight in the Lord, and he will give you your heart's desires.

Psalm 37:4

"I want it so bad I can taste it." Have you ever felt that way? Since my high school graduation, I truly had a desire to be the director of my old high school drill team. I would have walked to the ends of the earth and back, swum the widest sea, done whatever it took and yelled, "Pretty please with sugar on top!"

Of course those clichés are a bit of an exaggeration, but seriously, doing that job was something that I *really* wanted to do. However, as much as I wanted it, I didn't get the job. The job opening came and was snatched up. Just like that.

Hey, wait just a second there, God! What do you think you're doing? Have you ever given God attitude? I did. After all, I was delighting myself in him, praying and seeking his will; I truly thought that

God's guidance was moving me towards that particular job position. I followed the yellow brick road of my dreams right up to this opportunity, just to have the big iron gate slammed shut in my face.

So what's my point? I say all of this in order to tell you that in hindsight, I am so very grateful to God for knowing what is best for me. I have praised him time and time again since this so-called disappointment in my life. As a result of it, he has blessed me with some incredible experiences that I never would have known if that job had become mine. During the four years since then, God has given me some amazing girls to work with. And I have traveled to Europe, worked on this book, paid off my college loans and made some new friends, including the lady who got the very job that I had wanted. She and I even got to work together for a year. As I grew through the aftermath of this situation, I endured the testing, twisting, poking and prodding until I finally learned why God's answer to my prayers is always better than my own.

As teenagers, and even as adults, we struggle with what it really means to have the desires of our heart. There is a misconception many people have that goes something like this: getting the desires of my heart means getting what I want. As a teenager, I wanted to have a car, a boyfriend, money to spend on cool clothes and acceptance into a great college. I thought that getting those things would define who I was.

But as an adult, I find that as my heart becomes more aligned with God's heart, my desires change to more closely resemble his. I don't really care what kind of car I drive; instead I hope that all of the people I care about will drive safely and be protected. I don't care so much about having any boyfriend, but more about having the right boyfriend and eventually the right husband. I prefer not to spend so much money on clothes; I'd rather pay off my college loans and begin saving for my future. I realized after college that God expects so much more of my life than what I do with the job that my college degree provided for me. I do understand the meaning of disappointment. It isn't easy to weather a rejection, particularly when you are hardworking, focused on God and deserving of the things you desire—when your desires are godly and your motives are pure. But disappointment is temporary, and eventually healing does occur.

As I learn to delight myself daily in the Lord, I learn why God does not grant certain desires of mine. It is my prayer to be in the very center of God's will—to make sure that my thoughts are his thoughts, my actions his actions and my desires his desires. As these things begin to match up with God's, we often let go of things we never dreamed we would. But if you are seeking God's will for your life, you won't think twice. Go ahead, I dare you. Delight yourself—not in your own plans, but in God's, because you never know what he has in store!

Anything But Plastic

1. Psalm 37:4 seems like the perfect verse! But do you think that walking with God and receiving his gifts are as easy as just asking and receiving?

2. Read Psalm 145:18, 19. What do these verses say God does?

   If I asked you what the desires of your heart are at this point regarding talents, education, guys, career choice and your ministry in Christ, what would you say? Don't sugarcoat your answers or try to make them sound more spiritual. Your dreams and desires—what are they? Fire away!

   Do you think these desires will change as you get older? Why or why not?

3. Take a look at some other aspects of God's provision. Read the following verses and list some things that God provides for you or desires to provide for you. You may have to think a little bit. Don't just look for a gift that is visible; look for answers of a more spiritual nature.

   James 1:5:

   Psalm 21:1-6:

Philippians 1:6, 9, 10:

4. Read Ephesians 2:10. Why were you created? What good things have you been able to do already?

5. Your desires may not always be to do good things. Read Proverbs 16:1-3, 9. Have you ever made plans and then had things go a different way? How did you feel about that? Why do you think that happened?

What do you need to do to have plans that succeed?

Beyond Plastic . . . .

So many of your desires come from God. The question is, are you willing to have your patience, love, purity, character and other inner traits worked on, in order to show God that you are faithful enough to receive what he has for you?

It is amazing that when you pray for his qualities to be instilled in you and for him to help you to be in the center of his will, he gradually changes your desires to match his. Pray and ask God to direct your desires to the things he has prepared for you.

DISTORTED IMAGES

And so, dear brothers and sisters, I plead with you to give your bodies to God. Let them be a living and holy sacrifice—the kind he will accept. When you think of what he has done for you, is this too much to ask?

Romans 12:1

As the front door slams, an emaciated figure moves breathlessly across the room and stands in front of a full-length mirror. Returning from a strenuous run through the neighborhood, this girl with thin hair pulled away from her face closely examines herself in the glass. She wraps her bony fingers around her waist. When they fail to quite meet in front and back, she becomes panic-stricken at how overweight she appears. Do you know this girl?

How about this one? She looks normal to the average eye. But once the door shuts, the girl heads to the kitchen, gathers up an armful of whatever looks good from the cabinet and refrigerator, stuffs herself with as much food as she can gorge and then runs to her bathroom.

Only minutes later, the water runs to muffle first the sounds of forced vomiting and then the rustling of the wrappers on the laxative tablets as she tries to get rid of everything she just ate.

Are these girls your friends? People you know or worry about? Girls you see at school? Or maybe these scenarios hit closer to home. Perhaps I just described *you*. In our plastic world, you see pictures of slender people as you flip through your latest copies of *Teen*® magazine and *Vogue*®. Do you wonder if you could ever look like these images of thinness? Or do you believe that you *should* look like that, but feel guilty because you don't? I don't really know the two girls that I described earlier. But I know their demons—eating disorders such as anorexia and bulimia.

This eating disorder thing hits very close to home for me. Not only do I, as a dance teacher, see a number of girls who suffer from these eating disorders, but I know firsthand that anorexia and bulimia are diseases that teenagers in this generation see pretty much every day. When I notice girls struggling with these illnesses, bitter memories take me back to my own experimentation with anorexia.

I was walking the dangerous pathway toward being anorexic my sophomore year in high school. I know the pressure that comes with the sickness—the false idea that you have to look a certain way, be a perfect weight, wear an ideal size to get people to notice you in order to feel good about yourself. Maybe you base your whole self-confidence on your looks alone! Maybe you're thinking that looking like your favorite model or actress is the only way a guy will ever like you.

I know how it is. During my struggles with anorexia, I allowed these outside pressures to totally change the person that I wanted to become. Even though I knew deep down that my family loved me, that I had great friends who accepted me as I was and that I really was *not* fat, somehow that wasn't good enough. I continued to abuse my body and starve it of the nourishment that it needed. I got so caught up in how I looked that Satan had me right where he wanted me. I allowed him to distract me from the simple fact that God loves me—*no matter what.*

I eventually figured something out. Although God loves me regardless of what I do and what I look like, he also expects me to be responsible for my actions. I suddenly became very aware that it wasn't my body I was screwing up. My body is supposed to be his. Not just select parts that I choose to give over to him, but the whole thing—100 percent his. He asks us in his Word to offer our bodies as living sacrifices—holy and *pleasing* to him.

Oops . . . I'd missed that word *pleasing* before. As I look back now, I know that what I offered God was not a pleasing gift—a skinny body with a grumbling stomach, my period messed up because I caused it to stop, not to mention my shot self-esteem. I finally looked into the mirror one day and I just knew. The self-inflicted abuse to my body could in no possible way be making God happy. Some temple I had going!

Maybe you abuse your body in some way, doing what God never intended your body for. That could mean overeating as well as undereating, or just eating all junk food. Maybe you smoke, mess around with drugs or experiment with premarital sex.

Perhaps you let your body get so freaked out with worldly pressures that you have become depressed or stressed, which abuses your mental health. Whatever the dilemma, God wants to take care of it. He wants to help you release it to him so he can move back into his temple and start redecorating. He wants your whole body as his temple. He wants to hang out in all compartments of your heart, not just the select parts that *you* open to him. This relinquishing of your entire body to his reign is *not* a choice. We don't give our bodies over to Christ if and when we feel like it; we do it because he asks us.

Truthfully, I'm shocked that Christ has anything to do with me at all. He could just as easily overlook me for other people—those who are better, prettier, older and wiser, younger and more innocent or holier than I am. I'm messed up, but he wants to live with me and inside me! That's why I struggle constantly to wash the junk out of my body—to get rid of the physical and spiritual things that do not please him. I can already name several things I have thought or said about my body today that don't please God. I have to start cleaning house and getting ready for company. How about you?

Anything But Plastic

1. People abuse their own bodies in numerous ways. Some have more severe effects than others, but they are all bad. In what ways have you abused your body? Be honest and up-front with yourself.

2. What effect do these activities have on you, or how did they affect you in the past, physically, mentally and spiritually?

3. How do teen and fashion magazines make you feel about yourself when you look at them? If you feel they don't affect you much, think for a moment like the world thinks. List at least five standards you think the media tells you that you've got to meet in order to be successful and attractive.

4. Turn in the Bible to Romans 12:1, 2. What type of sacrifice is your body supposed to be? What will happen when you give your body to God? What will you know?

5. Read 1 Corinthians 6:19, 20. What is your body? Who does your body belong to? Why should you honor God?

Beyond Plastic . . . .

Do you honestly glorify God with your body? We all do in some ways. Think of ways you serve God with your body. (For example, do you praise him with your voice?)

Are there some parts of your temple that are not set apart for God, like your mouth, your weight or how you dress? Ask God now, honestly and specifically, to help you cleanse that part of your body for him. Ask him to help you see yourself through his eyes, not the world's.

FATAL FLAW?

*You made all the delicate, inner parts of my body
and knit me together in my mother's womb.*

Psalm 139:13

Pretty much every one of us was born with That Flaw—that one part of our bodies we believe is absolutely fatal.

We'd change it if we could. We may try to place the blame on genetics: "I can't help it—I got it from my mom," "The flat chest came from Dad's side!" or "I don't know where I got them—even my grandmother doesn't have big hips!" You can fill in the family member and the cursed body part! We've all got one—or several. Nevertheless, we're still God's unique creations, flaws and all!

My main area of concern, or should I say obsession, is my thighs. They're quite muscular, and seeing as I've been dancing since the age of three, I'm afraid they're here to stay. In typical girl fashion, sometimes I try to mentally recreate my body. I think

I've figured it out! Maybe if my hips were narrower, my legs wouldn't look as big, and then they wouldn't bother me as much; or if my face were a little wider, then my nose would not look so bony. It's obnoxious, really, the amount of time we spend analyzing our supposed flaws.

And it doesn't stop with our own bodies. I've even gone so far as to change the criteria of what I'm looking for in a guy because of my thoughts on physical appearance. My desire for him to be a godly man and a spiritual leader has, at times, slipped from priority number one on the list to make room for my new rules:

1. He must have bigger thighs than me.
2. He may not wear unfashionable jeans.

OK, all kidding aside! Real, spiritual leadership is much more important to me than what a guy's legs look like or what clothes he has hanging in his closet. And my personal relationship with Christ is much more important than what my own legs look like!

God tells me in Psalm 139 that I was knit together with love in my mother's womb. He tells me that he knows the things that I think about, the things that concern me or bother me, before I can even mention them. My natural response to God's infinite care and concern over my life should really be to give thanks to him, because I was delicately and wonderfully made just the way he desired me to be. Verse 14 tells me that his works are complex and awesome. These muscular legs and childbearing hips that I carry around with me are—somehow—wonderful!

When I have felt sorry for myself or been depressed about my body, I have tried to change my perspective. Instead of wallowing, I have tried praising God for my legs, thanking him that I can even walk, let alone dance, and that I can praise him with this bodily instrument. My heavenly Father reminds me that I am truly beautiful in his sight. The evidence is all around—but choosing to accept his compliment is up to me.

What do you view as your fatal flaw? Is your nose too big? rear end heading in the wrong direction? Are your hips too wide? love handles too lovable? When is the last time you actually *thanked* God for that "gift"? Do you ever think that this physical flaw might make it possible for you to minister to those around you?

You were born from a blank canvas that now bears your unique image. Your whole being, imperfections and all, are God's signature on his masterpiece. So the next time that negative self-perception sneaks up, try to thank God for who you are instead of whining about what you look like or don't look like. His works are marvelous!

Anything But Plastic

1. Before you start this week's study questions, read through Psalm 139 once or twice. Underline specific passages that help you. You might even try reading it out loud as a prayer or conversation with God and fill in your own name where it says "me" or "I." What lines mean the most to you?

2. One dictionary defines *flaw* in two ways.

   flaw: a break, scratch or crack that spoils something; a blemish
   flaw: a defect, error

   What do we usually do with a mirror or a glass when we break it? What typically happens to a model when she gains weight? What do you attempt to do when you have a horrendous zit on your face? In other words, what do we do with things that are flawed?

3. What do you consider to be your physical and emotional flaws or defects? Why do you think these things bother you?

Does God view these flaws the same way you do or the world does? Does he throw you away like a broken mirror, view you as washed-up, or cover you up like a big ugly zit and consider you totally useless?

4. You know the answers to those questions. No, no and no! Of course he doesn't! Not only does God not abandon you because of these flaws, he adopts you as his child. Read 1 Peter 1:18, 19. Knowing the price God has paid for you, what do you think your worth is in his eyes? How can you go about seeing yourself as God sees you?

Beyond Plastic . . . .

Pray right now to see yourself through God's eyes. Ask him to help you accept these traits that you find less than satisfying and use these gifts to glorify and serve him.

Memorize the parts of Psalm 139 that encourage you, and quote them when Satan begins to attack your perception of yourself. Better yet, memorize the whole psalm. I can tell you, doing that has been such an encouragement to me!

FEAR FACTOR

And the peace I give isn't like the peace the world gives.
So don't be troubled or afraid.

John 14:27

I once went to a picnic with a really nice setup. It looked like a giant playground, but for adults. There were two trampolines, a swimming pool, a sand volleyball pit, some hammocks for lounging, a table full of snacks and treats, and a wide-open space for playing football. But the biggest attraction of all was an old rope swing down by the pasture. The swing itself was not that large; the tire you sat on was more like a tricycle tire than that of a car. However, the problem at hand was not the size of the swing, but rather its location. As I stood next to the swing, I was basically at eye level with the tire as it dangled 4 feet above the ground.

It quickly became evident that getting on the swing would take a circus act rather than the simple task of just hopping on and having someone give me a push. Mounting the tire required the swinger to climb a ladder up a tree to a tiny platform about 25 feet above the ground. I am telling you, this was no ordinary tree swing!

As people looked on from the ground, daring souls climbed up one by one to attempt the death-defying feat of mounting the rope swing. When I could no longer stand to watch from the ground, I assumed my position on the platform, trembling with fear. Once I arrived at the top, however, my work had just begun. For the next step I had to drop a rope from the platform to someone who stood at the bottom of the tree. They then attached my rope to the tire swing that was on another tree some feet away. Next, as if being that high off of the ground weren't scary enough, I had to draw the swing up to the platform on my own.

The whole time I did so, I was kicking myself for climbing the dumb tree in the first place and seriously considering the option of wimping out and climbing back down the ladder to safety. Fear overwhelmed me. All I could see was the blur of the leaves on the ground far below. What if I fell? What if I jumped to get on the swing and missed? The view down there provided no encouragement.

But then I grasped the tire in my hands and stood up, facing my next challenge of actually getting onto the swing. I held the rope tightly in front of me, took one last look at the tire and held my breath. With a little hop and a prayer, I hurled myself off of the platform and planted my rear onto the tire as I leapt away from my sturdy footing. My heart pounded with the success of my stunt, and I felt the exhilaration and freedom of swinging through the air! I now know that I would not have forgiven myself if I had left the picnic without experiencing the rush of the rope swing.

I can't tell you how often I take my eyes off of Christ and stubbornly cast them downward. Immediately anxiety and fear follow. I have no clue what lies ahead, I don't feel in control of the difficult situation, and I want to back out of my problem and cower out of the dilemma like I almost did with the rope swing.

But what an amazing thing it is to regain focus on Christ when my eyes move to him and I no longer fear. I don't ever want to miss out on the exhilaration of receiving God's peace. What good comes from looking down, when I just lose sight of him? I want to swing in faith instead of cowering in fear. Come on! What a rush!

Anything But Plastic

. . . .

1. What would you say that you are most afraid of right now?

2. What happens to your relationship with Christ when you are afraid? What is your attitude and what tends to be the focus of your prayers when you fret?

3. Read the following: Psalm 27:1; Isaiah 41:10. Why should you not fear, according to these verses?

4. You have looked at God's commands for you *not* to be afraid, but take a look at Psalm 34:9; 1 Samuel 12:24. What do these verses instruct you to do?

What do you think is meant by the phrase "fear God"?

5. Why do Christians ever fear or worry about things? What do you think is missing or perhaps becomes weak in a Christian's life that might allow unhealthy fear in?

Read Luke 17:5. Even the apostles needed more faith at times. When have you needed more faith? What did you do?

In closing, read Proverbs 31:30. What is a quality of a beautiful and godly woman that causes her to be praised?

Beyond Plastic . . . .

Each time you fear in a worldly way, stop and ask God for the faith to believe in him. The only fear that's good to have is a healthy respect and love for God. So, eyes up! Focus on him and don't be afraid!

A SLAP IN THE FACE

When I was growing up, people always taught me that this verse meant that when someone hurt my feelings, I was supposed to forgive them and somehow get over it. It was not until a few summers ago that I learned the literal meaning of this verse, and there was no symbolism to figure out!

While traveling to France that summer, I visited a little hot spot in the south called Nice (pronounced like "niece," in case you don't know). There's an old saying that "Nice is nice"—I'm not so sure I can back that one up. I don't think I'll be visiting again anytime soon, because my memories of this resort city are bittersweet. One evening, my cousin and I took a walk along a famous boulevard just across from the beach. We were laughing, talking, taking in the sights and minding our own business—or at least, I was pretty sure we were.

When I looked away from a beachfront building, a young woman caught my eye. She was probably about my age, maybe younger. She was wearing a folksy type of outfit—a white, frilly blouse and a red skirt with ruffles on the bottom—and carried a basket of roses on her arm. It was a little out of place for the beach, but I thought, *Cool, maybe she works at some neat little ethnic restaurant.* She was a tiny thing who seemed completely harmless. She was certainly not anyone I thought would cause me any trouble. I mean, please—ruffles and roses?—she was the epitome of sweetness and sunshine. But I guess I was wrong! She was obviously headed home after a hard day's work, in the restaurant or selling her flowers, when out of the middle of nowhere she stuck out her arm and slapped me!

Yeah, you got it! She slapped me—right across my face! You may be thinking, *You've got to be kidding.* That's certainly what I thought! I stopped dead in my tracks, and after the momentary shock wore off, I turned to my cousin, not sure whether to laugh or to cry.

"Did you see that? That girl just slapped me!" I think my cousin was as dumbfounded as I was.

Because our mystery flower girl had been walking in the opposite direction, I turned around expecting to find her laughing or coming to offer an apology. Fat chance. She was casually walking away without so much as a glance over her shoulder, an apology or even a smile. I was thinking that someone had to be playing a joke on me.

I'd like to give you the Christian answer and say that I stopped right there and said a prayer for her, or that I forgave her the way Christ would do. But my gut reaction was not the most flattering. I wanted to run after her, trip her and slap her too. I have to admit that, in my rage, I even felt like cussing her out. Even though that slap physically stung my cheek all evening long, the biggest pain I suffered was trying to figure out why in the world

she had hit me. Was I laughing too loudly? Had I committed some cultural no-no or made some crude body gesture? Or did she just not like the way I looked? Was my fair Irish skin a little too pale for the tan beach goddess of Nice? I could come up with nothing logical, and I gave up trying to figure it out. Although I was angry then, I laugh about it now.

Has this ever happened to you? Maybe you haven't been literally slapped across the face, but have you ever *felt* like you have been slapped? Maybe someone teased you for a physical trait, a habit or a belief that you possess. Perhaps someone betrayed you by sharing something personal that they swore they'd keep secret. Maybe someone lied to you, misquoted you or told a lie about you. Although these things affect our emotions, they can sting just like a physical slap.

I have been hurt by other people—the kind who laugh at you and talk about you behind your back. I've been just as hurt when people ignored me and completely left me out of the group. What motivates people to act like this is sometimes incomprehensible. But then God never promises to give us a complete understanding of *why* he allows these sorts of things to happen to us. We just have to dust off our pride, suck it up and go on with life.

What he does tell us, however, is that our response to these unexplained circumstances should be to turn the other cheek. Just this week I had an adult do something to me that made me feel dumb and unimportant. I've had to ask God four or five times to help me control my emotion and get over it. I was mad. But when people hurt us, we've got to respond to them the way God would want.

It's OK to allow people to see you vulnerable and upset. Show them you are human; it's OK for them to see you cry or be disappointed. But what they must never see is you reacting in anger to pay them back with their own methods. If you just allow them to see your humility, God can be so much more obvious to them through you. When we fight back, repaying people evil for evil and opening our big mouths, we always get in the way of the work that God desires to do through us.

So if the slap hurts and the sting is strong, just keep walking and laugh it off. For when you suffer with a controlled spirit, you are made more like Christ and others will be able to see him in you.

Anything But Plastic

1. Have you ever been deliberately hit or physically wounded? Summarize the situation.

2. Maybe you haven't been hit physically. But what about the other kind of slap we read about in today's study? Most everyone has suffered the sting of being falsely accused of something, spoken about unkindly or treated in any other of the ways teenagers so often hurt one another. What was a "slap" that caused you pain? Describe it.

3. How did you respond to that pain? What were your emotional, physical and verbal reactions?

4. As uncomfortable as it may be to recall, has there ever been a time when *you* have been the one to deliver a painful "slap" to someone you know or love? What did you say or do to cause that person pain? What was the person's reaction?

5. Read Hebrews 10:30. Summarize the content of the verse in your own words.

Also read Deuteronomy 32:35, 36. In your opinion, is it easy not to want to take revenge? Why or why not? How can you prepare yourself to respond in a godly manner the next time someone hurts you?

Beyond Plastic . . . .

You never know when a slap might hit you out of the blue! Pray now that God will prepare you to respond daily as he would in all situations.

GOOD TIMES, BAD TIMES

Enjoy prosperity while you can. But when hard times strike, realize that both come from God. That way you will realize that nothing is certain in this life.

Ecclesiastes 7:14

Have you ever experienced one of those days that are so *unbelievably* messed up that you don't know whether to laugh or to cry? I'm talking about the kind of day where you get to the end of it all and think, *Surely the joke's on me!*

Not too long ago, the joke was definitely on me. It was a Saturday morning during a difficult time in my life. It's amazing how God chooses to teach us lessons when the chips are down! I had just come through several stressful months: I had to make some tough, emotionally draining decisions; my parents faced difficulties; and my sister's family was dealing with health problems. I think everyone was in desperate need of a vacation.

In order to give my sister a break, my parents had volunteered to spend the night with the three grandkids while my sister and her husband went away for the weekend. That's the setup. Now here's how my incredibly messed-up Saturday unfolded.

I call my parents at the grandkids' house to check on them. Mom has a migraine and is throwing up. Meanwhile, the air conditioner in Mom and Dad's house has broken and is dumping water everywhere. Dad returns to their home to let the dog out. The living room carpet is soaking wet. Dad calls the repairman to hurry out. Dad calls me to see if I can go relieve my puking mother. I can't do it. I am supposed to be at work but volunteer to drop lunch off to the kids. En route, and about to lose it completely, I get a call from Dad on my cell. I ask him why God lets everything happen at once. Dad gives wise counsel to hang in and trust God. I head for a fast-food lunch pickup. A mile down the road, I see this big blur outside the car window in my peripheral vision and then . . .

Have you ever had fifty thoughts fly through your head all at once? The thoughts are coming so fast, yet the situation seems to be happening in slow motion. Picture that sensation.

What's that?! Oh my gosh! It's a deer! What's it doing in the suburbs at noon? It's coming straight at me! I can't stop! She won't stop! We're going to hit! What do I do?! Close your eyes! It's not happening if you close your eyes!

I close my eyes. According to the jolt I experience, I just know that I've run over her. Oh no, I'm a Bambi-smusher! But when I open my eyes, it turns out that she's run over *me*! The doe has attempted to hurdle my car and has plowed into my front windshield instead! The window is caved in just inches from my face, and I am covered in glass from head to toe.

The saga continues as I call 911. The cops come, but don't stay long. They leave to chase down a hit-and-run driver. (Guess it doesn't matter that I've just suffered from a hit-and-run!) My dad can't come get me because he's waiting on the repair guy. And I can't call anyone else to help,

because apparently 911 puts a block on calls made from cell phones. So, I'm left sitting alone on the side of the road, while the kids are going hungry and my mom's still hurling! Stop the madness!

To make a long story short—I survived surprisingly unharmed, apart from a few glass cuts! On a day like that—which I now call a "deer day"—I have to stop and say, "God, you've got to be kidding!"

Ecclesiastes 7:14 says that God allows days like these as a reminder to us that only he knows what each day will bring. He wants to keep us on our toes! Sure, we make plans and schedule things for days, weeks or even years to come. And God may have some of these same plans in mind for you. In fact I believe that if you are truly following his will, God's plans and your plans will become one and the same, or else he will change your heart to make them so. You may know for certain that you will go to college and then enter a certain career. But remember that between point A and point B, God may throw in some twists and turns— things you do not anticipate. He holds the compass and he will guide us through.

Messed-up days will come your way. Be ready for them. But grab those moments of happiness through the hard times, and by all means—laugh! God has a sense of humor, and so should we!

Anything But Plastic

1. Have you ever had a "deer day"—or even a week or month like that? What was the turn of events that came your way? Do you agree that God sometimes allows bad days to happen? Why do you think bad days do come?

2. We'll talk more about rotten days again later. But let's talk about good days first. Can you think of one of the best days of your life? Describe what happened in order to make the day awesome.

   Do you think God had anything to do with these good things? Why do you think he allows days of prosperity to happen to us?

3. Read 1 Kings 10:6-9. In these verses the Queen of Sheba tells Solomon that she admires him for several things. Name three things. Who does she give credit to for these blessings?

Now read Psalm 30:4-7, 11, 12. In verse 5, whose favor lasts for a lifetime? In verse 7, who made David as secure as a mountain?

4. Some people say that it is easier to praise God and worship him when things are going well. I sometimes feel the opposite. I tend to get too relaxed when days are good and I find it easier to cling to him when times are cloudy and uncertain. How do normal or good days affect you? What happens to your attitude and spirit when bad days come your way?

5. Read Jeremiah 22:21-23. What happened to the Israelites when they were prosperous? Do you think God at times messes with your comfort zone a bit, or a lot, in order to bring your focus back to him?

There are people who believe that cancer, unexpected deaths and incidents such as 9/11 are proof that God doesn't love us. At times these people even believe that there is no God at all. Pulling from your own knowledge of God, how can you be ready to defend his actions to those who might accuse God of allowing bad things to happen to good people?

Beyond Plastic . . . .

How can you use your own "deer days" to be prepared to be a witness for Christ? I challenge you to see your incredibly messed-up days in a new light!

GOOD ENOUGH?

Dear friend, don't let this bad example influence you. Follow only what is good. Remember that those who do good prove that they are God's children, and those who do evil prove that they do not know God.

3 John 1:11

How many times can you recall when the act of being good truly paid off? Maybe when you were a little girl, your parents told you that Santa only brings presents to the good girls and boys. Were you sometimes rewarded with a treat if you behaved well while Mom or Dad accomplished some work? There are some instances when being good still pays off. Good grades and test scores often ensure your admission to college. In order to make the drill team, the cheerleading squad, first chair in band or the lead in a play, you must be good at that sport or fine art.

So, for a Christian, life ought to be a piece of cake, right? When confronted with a choice between good and bad, Christians usually choose what is good, don't they? But is "good" really good enough?

In 2 Thessalonians 1:11, we are told that we have been called to a high calling of faith. God not only calls us to walk in Christ, but he wants us to walk in Christ to the highest degree that is possible, which often means passing over what is *good* for what is *best*. In order to grow in your walk with Christ, you must truly seek God's best for you. Probably many of you are not easily tempted by Satan to do bad things; for you the struggle is not in avoiding bad decisions, but in making the best decisions.

At the end of my eighth grade year, my parents and I were confronted with an important decision. I could stay in the feeder program where I was, go into the neighborhood high school and remain with my old friends. My other option was to move to a nearby high school with exemplary academics, challenging extracurricular programs and total strangers. The first option would not have been a bad one, but I don't think I would be the same person I am today had I chosen it.

At my new high school, the bar of excellence was set high. The people I met influenced my life in ways that affect me to this day. Could God have chosen other teachers and friends to impact my life at the first school? Certainly, but after much prayer and consideration, God showed me that school number two was indeed the *best* one for me.

I remember several times in college when it was in my best interest to select an 8 AM class because the teacher was excellent. Truth be told, I would have loved an extra few hours of sleep, along with an easier teacher in the afternoon. I doubt that I would have failed in my academics if I had chosen to go to later classes, but the choice would not have been the *best*. God wanted to challenge me through those earlier classes and tougher teachers.

When I finished college and applied for teaching jobs, I truly believed God was calling me to work at a particular school. I interviewed there and then waited for the phone call. While I waited, I received two other job offers. Both were jobs that provided good opportunities. But were they the best for me? No, and as I held out, God blessed my patience by providing the *best* job for me.

To date, the biggest issue that confronts me still is that of waiting for the man I'm supposed to marry. God has allowed me to experience a few good relationships. But do I settle for something good? Or do I wait for God's best for me?

So, back to the question I asked at the beginning: Living the Christian life should be easy, right? Wrong! God will test you, because only by taking his tests, studying life's lessons and having our character shaken a bit, do we really become the people he desires that we be. Life is an awesome event if you really seek God's perfect will in any and every situation (big or little) that comes your way. Remember good is great, but better is best!

Anything But Plastic

1. New Christians often start out struggling between good and bad. As you grow deeper in your faith, it becomes less tempting to do what is bad. What events or trials have you encountered as a Christian (regardless of how they turned out) when you have been confronted by making a decision of good versus best?

2. For each of the decisions you listed above, do you think you made the right decision? Why or why not? And if so, what fruits and blessings did you see in your life as a result of each right decision?

3. Sometimes you may feel like you don't have the power to follow through in doing the best things. Read 2 Corinthians 13:3, 4. How do you think knowing that God's power is at work in you can help you do what's best?

4. Read Jeremiah 29:11. What do you think God has in store for you when you are obedient to him and choose *best*, rather than just *good*?

Beyond Plastic...

Remember, good is great, but better is best! Take the challenge today to go for the best in your life. Don't settle for anything less!

WHAT'S THE 411?

> *Besides, they are likely to become lazy and spend their time gossiping from house to house; getting into other people's business and saying things they shouldn't.*
>
> *1 Timothy 5:13*

Let's look at two different aspects of laziness. To start, we will take a look at the teenage girl's biggest temptation to laziness: gossiping! Yep! I said gossiping. I know you're thinking, *I thought laziness was when you sat around like a slacker doing nothing!*

And you're right. That's part of it, but there's more to it than that! Lazy people don't *really* want to just sit around doing nothing. They're looking for something to do all right, but when they channel that energy into actual activity, it's bad news! Lazy females often become gossiping females—also known as busybodies. I'd say some of us have got it down to an art form!

I'm sure that at some point in your life, you've played a game called Grapevine. Or you may call it Telephone. Regardless of the name, the rules are the same: start a message at one point in a circle and see how messed up it gets by the time it travels from whisper to whisper to the very last person in the circle. I know, part of the fun for some players is to screw up the message on purpose. But no matter how you play it, "Jason Johnson is hot and has gorgeous blue eyes!" can turn into "Sarah Swanson is a snot and gets all of the guys." As the message gets butchered all around the circle, laughter breaks forth from some players. Then tears begin to roll down someone's face as the final message is proclaimed: "Lacey Lawson smokes pot and has thunder thighs!"

Something that starts out as a joke can quickly become damaging as girls do one of the evil things they do best—get involved in everybody else's business and spread rumors around! All it takes is overhearing the tail end of a conversation or typical locker room talk to ignite the rapid, wildfire-like spreading of rumors, lies and distorted truths. Soon there are people freaking out all over the place. When I was growing up, I had several friends my mom warned me not to tell *anything* to if I didn't want it splashed around the school. She always said, "Telephone, telegraph, tell _____, tell *all*!" You can fill in the blank with the best busybody you know from your circle of friends.

I know most of you don't relate to this busybody thing! You *never* get involved in gossipy lunchroom chat. You wouldn't dare exaggerate any part of someone else's conversation or jump to conclusions after hearing only bits and pieces of something. You don't just listen in on negative talk without standing up for the person being talked about. Right?

But remember—it all goes back to laziness. When we have too much time on our hands, we are bound to find ourselves involved in something negative. I hate to sound like a self-help guru, but if we don't invest our time in positive activities, we're going down, and sometimes we take someone with us. If we can't resist a negative comment among a group of friends, we need to move on down the hallway. If we aren't going to defend the person being spoken about, we need to head to class early. Look for someone who might need a *positive* comment and encourage her!

I know we might have the gift of gab, but God is very specific as to what he does and does not want us gabbing about. Ephesians 4:29 says, "Don't use foul and abusive language." Ouch! That hurts me just a bit. Even if we don't say it out loud, the negative comments are often burning on the tips of our tongues. Almost every day brings some sort of gossip or jealous word to our hot little mouths. We may feel momentary relief when we say it, but all in all, is gossip really worth the pain, disappointment or hurt feelings that it causes?

How do you spend your free time? Do people blaze a trail to you with the 411, because they know you will want to know? Are you a Telephone kind of girl? The gift of gab God gave you is meant for more positive and uplifting things. Find a new game and let that messed-up message stop with you.

Anything But Plastic

. . . .

1. Read Proverbs 26:17–22. What do these verses compare the interfering act of gossip to? Why do you think that quarrels disappear when the gossip stops? Explain.

2. Have you ever heard the saying "Sticks and stones may break my bones, but words will never hurt me"? Is this even remotely true? Can you recall a time when words hurt you? Can you remember to this day what was said to or about you that hurt your feelings?

Read Proverbs 26:22 again. Where does this verse say rumors go? If you can still remember harmful gossip that someone has said about you, then believe that the same is true when you gossip about others!

How do you think the people you gossip about would feel if they knew what you were saying?

3. Read James 3:8. Who does this verse say can tame the tongue?

As humans, we are incapable of controlling this gossip-ridden part of our bodies on our own. Since it's impossible, does this mean we are free to work the grapevine as much as we feel like? Why or why not?

Who is the only one who can help you tame your tongue?

4. In closing, read Proverbs 25:11, 12. To what does verse 11 compare words that are spoken at the right time?

What can you do to break the chain of gossip? When the opportunity to gossip arises, what can you say to or about someone that could be like gold or silver instead of poison?

Beyond Plastic

Ask God to help you tame your tongue! Ask him to fill your mouth with words that glorify him and lift others up. He can turn poison into silver and gold.

KNOW YOUR AUDIENCE

Then each of you will control your body and live in holiness and honor—not in lustful passion as the pagans do, in their ignorance of God and his ways.

1 Thessalonians 4:4, 5

He is really hot! You've been watching him since the first day of school. Anytime he comes nearby, you get tongue-tied; you know he is after some other girl and has no clue that you even exist. And then one day he calls you, says he likes you and wants to take you out. You can't believe it! After several months of dating, you decide you like him even more. He even says he loves you and he would do anything for you. The question is, would you do anything to keep *him*? How far would you go to ensure that he's still yours? How far is OK? How far is too far?

Yes, I am talking about the taboo topic of sex and everything that leads up to it. By that, I mean anything you do that might lead to physical, lustful acts, where the body takes over the mind. This could

be innocent kissing that is taken a bit too far, touching or perhaps even more. When these things happen, your body takes control, and your mind becomes less able to make rational decisions quickly enough for you to pull yourself out of a potentially dangerous situation.

I know. This would never happen to you. You are too sensible, right? You know when to say when. Yeah, right!

I can relate to what you face. I am well aware of the fact that it is hard to be self-disciplined in the area of physical desires. Let's face it—things of the flesh feel good! God knows this too, which is why he wants to save you from turning this good gift into terrible temptation.

Every time sexual temptation has come my way, I have had to make an effort to possess myself. But I have realized with time that although the physical feels good, relationships built on physical acts don't last.

That doesn't mean that I don't long for the physical in the proper context. Don't get me wrong! But I know that God meant for these things to be kept within marriage for a reason. Relationships must be based on friendship and love for Christ if they are going to last. And having sex outside of marriage, *not* loving Christ and his commands, always ends up damaging that relationship with Christ and hurting everyone involved.

But how do you know when you've crossed the line? Let me ask you this. Have you ever done something, and even though you knew nobody saw it, you felt horrible and couldn't get your mind off the situation? That's actually a good thing. That feeling is the Holy Spirit convicting you, because someone did see what you did—Jesus did! Even though his presence is not detectable physically, he is powerful, he knows everything and he is always watching.

My mom's dad (my "Papa") once gave her a piece of advice, which she passed down to me. First we need to pray continually that God will help us keep our actions pure and lead us away from situations that might require us to make hasty decisions. And secondly, as Papa used to say, we need to remember that Jesus is with us at all times as our audience. So there's the answer. If the action we are faced with is something we wouldn't want Jesus to see, then it is wrong. There is no question. Don't do it! Forget how the act makes us feel physically or emotionally. Forget what the boy says and the warm fuzzies that accompany those words.

Do you really want to do things that make God cringe and hang his head in disappointment? If you have had to question your actions, chances are you already know the type of behavior that is acceptable with a guy. I can tell you that it is possible to maintain your virginity. I've been where you are, but through God's grace and protection, he has helped me save myself even to the ripe old age of thirty-two! Believe it or not, it can be done!

Anything But Plastic

1. Sure, you live in a different society to that of biblical times. But do you think God has changed or lowered his standard for you regarding sex to match the standards of the world today?

   Read 1 Corinthians 6:18–20 and answer the following questions. What does verse 18 tell you to run away from?

   How does verse 19 refer to your body? Who lives inside the temple of your body?

   Do you belong to yourself? What sacrifice did God make to buy you? What should you do with your body?

2. What do you think are the effects of lustful acts and sexual acts that are done outside of marriage? How do they affect God?

3. Read John 1:5–9. Who is the true light? How does it make you feel to know that Jesus sees all the things that you do and that you can't hide anything in the darkness from him?

4. Read 1 Thessalonians 4:3-5. Why does God want you to keep clear of sexual immorality?

Why, according to verse 5, do the pagans live their lives in lustful passion?

How are you doing with the upkeep of your temple? Have you given it over to someone it doesn't belong to?

5. Read Song of Songs 2:7. What does this verse say should not be woken up until the time is right?

Read Song of Songs 4:12. What is the writer referring to when he talks about his love being a private garden or spring?

Do you have your desires under control? What is it that you want to do differently in this area of your life?

Beyond Plastic . . . .

Surrender this area of your life to God. If you've made mistakes, he will renew you. All you have to do is confess to him, and he will put his seal of protection over each and every one who presents her innocence to him. He will help you guard yourself until the time is right.

WHERE ARE YOU FROM?

The land you have given me is a pleasant land.
What a wonderful inheritance!

Psalm 16:6

What is your heritage? If you are anything like I was at your age, you would respond to that question with the usual "Huh?" What I mean is, where are your ancestors from? How did your family end up in the United States? Where do your family traditions stem from? If you can't even begin to answer my questions, then I challenge you to find the answers. Dig in! Go exploring! Go on a treasure hunt for valuable prizes that you will never regret finding.

My quest for my heritage began seven or so years ago when Riverdance exploded onto the scene and ignited a craze. I have been a dancer since the age of three, but after probing a bit deeper into the Irish style, I realized that the passion for this particular kind of dance was in my blood. You see, I'm Irish by heritage. I'm Scottish and Dutch as well. And there are characteristics within my temperament that are a result of my cultural background. The Irish are known for being passionate about their causes. Do you see what I'm getting at?

I have learned so much about my heritage since I began my personal treasure hunt. For instance, my long legs and sense of humor come from my dad; my grandmother unfortunately passed a flat chest down to me; my fascination with French culture, fine art, beautiful colors and anything created by hand comes from my mother and hers before her. My mom also gave me the curse of perfectionism. My love for old hymns comes from my grandfather Jackson who used to sing as he worked in his garden. My grandfather Phillips, who fought in World War II, passed down a strong patriotism for our country, and since his death several years ago, I've noticed my heritage jumping out at me from our family photos in ways that I've never experienced before.

I have walked past black–and–white pictures of my family hundreds of times before; but now they all look different. The eyes of my ancestors pierce me as if they hold great stories of our past that they long to share with me. My dad recently noticed a picture of Great-great-grandfather Calvin Arthur Hobbs, who had a receding hairline. He now believes he has found the cause of balding in our family!

There is a reason that your hair is the color it is or that you are drawn to a certain art or talent. There is a reason your grandmother cooks a dish a certain way. Instead of rolling your eyes and turning up the volume the next time your parents begin to talk about their childhood or something their grandmothers taught them, maybe you should sit up and hit the mute button instead. Listen to the stories of your heritage so that they don't get lost in the dust of your generation. Older people have wonderful memories and stories to share.

The verse from Psalm 16 above talks about land that has been passed down. Since I have not inherited any land, I see my beautiful lines of heritage as the people that I am related to for centuries back. I think it's so cool that I can look at an old photo and even without personal knowledge of my great-great grandmother know that I am a part of her, an extension of her, and I can one day teach my children about our shared heritage.

What about the thousands of years of spiritual heritage that you have? As a child of Christ, when you become part of his family you become a spiritual heir with David, Abraham, Mary, Job and the many others we can read about in Scripture. Perhaps you have wisdom like Solomon or you doubt like Thomas. Maybe you are brave like David and fearless like Daniel. Look into the spiritual eyes of Scripture and delve into those "photo albums." Discover where it is that you came from. Aren't you just a little bit curious to know your heritage?

Anything But Plastic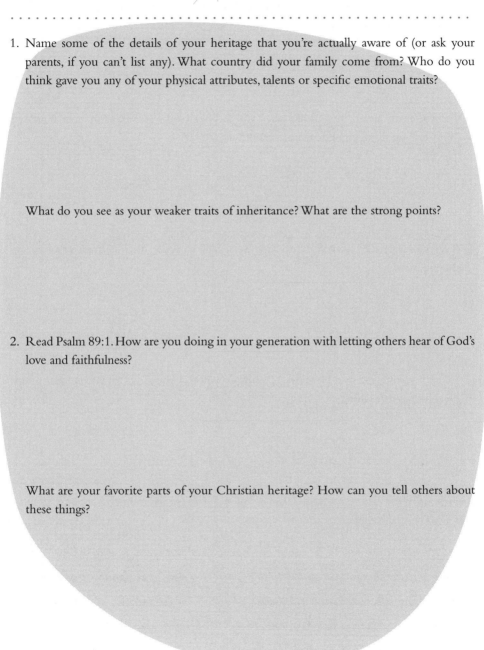

1. Name some of the details of your heritage that you're actually aware of (or ask your parents, if you can't list any). What country did your family come from? Who do you think gave you any of your physical attributes, talents or specific emotional traits?

   What do you see as your weaker traits of inheritance? What are the strong points?

2. Read Psalm 89:1. How are you doing in your generation with letting others hear of God's love and faithfulness?

   What are your favorite parts of your Christian heritage? How can you tell others about these things?

3. In 1 Corinthians 3, Paul talks about our foundation in Jesus Christ. Read verses 10-15. If you neglect the very gifts and qualities God has given you, the foundation he has laid for you, he might shake up your life a bit to see how your building stands. How do you think your work would stand up to the fire right now?

Can you name a time in your life when you feel like God was shaking up your building? What do you think you learned as a result?

4. Read Colossians 1:11-14. What do these verses tell us about the inheritance that we are sharing in?

Take some time and read Hebrews 11. How do you feel knowing that you are part of this great heritage of faith?

Beyond Plastic . . . .

What do you want people to remember about you and your family name? Think of some specific things you would like to pass on from your family regarding your spiritual life, emotional attributes, physical traits, talents, abilities and other qualities. Make a list here and check back every now and then to remind yourself to pass on that excellent heritage!

JUST BECAUSE

For he himself has said, "You must be holy because I am holy."

1 Peter 1:16

Do you feel like being a teenager is next to impossible—as if nobody truly understands how you feel? Do you feel like adults always find you guilty of something and think that you don't really know anything because of your age? All grown-ups want to do is talk down to you. And your parents! I know—don't even get you started, right? What do they know about being a teenager in this day and age, anyway?

How many times do you disagree with your parents? Do you think they are just a little bit too strict? Does it seem like all of your friends stay out later than you? Do their parents permit them to go places that yours don't? Life is just so unfair, and your parents refuse to see your side. And I know—the one that really gets you is

when you ask your parents for a reason why they call the shots the way they do, and they respond with that slick answer, "Just because I said so!"

I know you won't like what I am about to say, but do you know that maybe your parents are not so far off the mark? It's true—being a teenager is a tough job, and sometimes being a Christian is not any easier. A genuine walk with Christ can be tiresome. At times it's frustrating, aggravating and an absolute chore. There are so many times that I ask God the same things you might ask your parents: "Why? Why won't you let me do such and such? Why must I do *this*? Why should I be obedient to you if it will only cause me pain? It would be so much easier to just do it another way. Surely people won't notice if I respond in a less Christlike manner."

The hardest thing for me to come to grips with is that a lot of the time God does not answer my questions or respond to my whining at all—or at least he doesn't appear to. God is under no obligation to tell me his reasoning behind the things that he allows to occur in my life. He is a sovereign God and may do as he pleases. Although it would be so much easier at times to give up on being a Christian, to lay down my armor and relax into a more worldly lifestyle, God reminds me that I must be holy, because he is holy. He does not tell me to be holy because it will help me in the future, because it will make people like me more or because I will achieve or acquire something faster than other people. He gives us that parental type of answer that is the most difficult for us to deal with: "Just because I said so."

As true followers of Christ, the fact that God tells us to be holy should be reason enough for us to obey him and to continue living as he calls us to do. In fact, we should be overjoyed at the opportunity to be shaped and molded within the lives that God allows us to live. And we have the perfect example of holiness before us.

Christ was the embodiment of holiness even in his earthly life as a man. After all, even he had parents that he had to obey!

For all of the times that making a Christlike decision is difficult, the choice of being a Christian is much more exciting than it is frustrating. Being a Christian brings such freedom. There is a release in knowing you have salvation, a companion who never forsakes you, a shepherd who protects you, an all-knowing God who has your whole future planned and a vinedresser who prunes you and shapes in you the qualities of love, joy, peace, patience and other Christlike attributes. So when God calls us to holiness, it should be a privilege rather than a chore. It's true that we will never fully understand God's ways. He is a mystery. But he is also infinitely trustworthy. So, keep up the work of being a committed Christian. Pursue holiness with a passion and accept the "just because" side of God. The freedom of walking in Christ far outweighs the frustration.

And by the way, that same God that sometimes doesn't respond to our questions also chooses to love us, not because we deserve it . . . but "just because"!

Anything But Plastic

1. Have you ever asked your parents to let you do something and they wouldn't let you? Why do you think they didn't let you? What were your attitude and reaction to their authority over you?

2. What about the same situation in your relationship with God? What have you desired or asked of him where you have gotten a "just because" answer? What is your attitude toward God when he responds this way?

3. You can get frustrated with God and still be in awe of him. I still find mystery in every sunset that I see. I can't see God with my eyes, but I can see him in his sunsets. That makes him intriguing and mysterious to me. What are some of the things about God that you find mysterious?

Write the best definition you can for the word *holy* below.

Read 1 Samuel 2:2. According to this verse, who is holy?

4. Read 1 Peter 1:14–16. What reasons can you find in these verses for being holy?

You are called to be holy, because you are a child of God, because you know it's right and just because God says so! Can we ever be totally holy? Not in this lifetime! And definitely never on our own. So why do you think it is important to strive for holiness? Read Philippians 2:3-11 and write down your answers.

Beyond Plastic . . . .

How is your "holiness meter" reading? Consider your actions, thoughts, words of your mouth and time spent with God. What areas do you think you could work on? Pray and ask God to help you with your quest to be more like him. Ask him to help you to see the quest for holiness as a privilege and not a chore. Ask him to help you relax in his "just because" responses and bask in his mystery.

CAN YOU HEAR HIM NOW?

This was his plan from all eternity, and it has now been carried out through Christ Jesus our Lord. Because of Christ and our faith in him, we can now come fearlessly into God's presence, assured of his glad welcome.

Ephesians 3:11, 12

Have you ever had this overwhelming sense that you needed to do something, and until you acted upon it, you felt miserable? I experienced this feeling one night at dinner. My parents and I went out to eat at a Mexican restaurant the night before I was scheduled to check in for ear surgery. Dinner out was supposed to distract me, relax me and keep my mind off of going under the knife.

It sort of worked, but from the moment we sat down, the dining experience was anything but relaxing. I couldn't help but be distracted by a middle-aged man at the bar who did nothing but yell at the two men next to him. I was certain that he was already sloshed as I watched him continue to drink and to smoke like a chimney. His voice and the content of his conversation became extremely audible across the restaurant. The annoying thing about it, other than the fact that he was very rude and old enough to know better, was the fact that every other word out of his mouth was the "f-word." Meanwhile his two sidekicks sat there dumbfounded, just taking the verbal beating. Also in the bar sat a lady with two little girls. I was shocked at the fact that no one in the restaurant had complained and that the management didn't seem to care. The young mother didn't even seem fazed by the language that her daughters were hearing.

The more I sat and listened, the angrier I became. At one point I said to my family, "I'm going to go talk to him," to which my dad responded, "No, I'll go; you stay here!"

My mom and I cringed at the thought of that happening, because my dad's temper has been known to flare when he feels strongly about something. But the nudging in my heart and mind did not go away. I knew I had to do something. Though I questioned what exactly that something might be, I also knew that this urge I felt came from the Holy Spirit and that I must do something if I wanted to respond with obedience. So I got up and walked to the bar, praying the whole time, "Heavenly Father, please help me know what to say," but thinking in the back of my mind, *I'm going to get killed!*

The walk from my table to the bar had that nightmarish quality of walking down a never-ending hallway to my doom. When I reached the men, it felt as if I stood there for hours before I was finally able to say, "Excuse me, sir. I don't mean to be rude; but I can hear you from clear across the restaurant, and what you are saying is very offensive to me. I would really appreciate it if you would be a little more quiet."

He stared back at me for a few seconds, and I waited to receive my beating. But it didn't come, so at last I turned and went back to my table.

Looking back, I realize that the only way I did what I did was through bold and confident access to the Holy Spirit. My action was entirely through his leading. Although responding to the Holy Spirit is an act of faith, in this case I did receive an immediate blessing from my obedience. A man at the table behind us said that he admired me for doing what I did. But I knew there was no need for me to be afraid, because I am promised boldness and confidence in Christ, particularly when I am obedient to him. Isn't it nice that when he calls us to do something, he equips us for the task?

Anything But Plastic

1. I often beat myself up for not being able to hear God's voice. But hearing the voice of God is maybe less common than the use of the phrase. Read Ephesians 4:22, 23 and then give a reason why we may not always hear God's voice.

2. After Jesus opened the way between you and God by being punished for your sins, he left his Holy Spirit so that he could communicate with you. However, in the Bible we read of several people to whom God actually spoke. What would your reaction be if God himself spoke to you?

3. The author Henry Blackaby, in his book *Experiencing God*, has made a list of four ways God talks to us today: through the Holy Spirit, other believers, his Word and circumstances.

   Describe a time when you felt the Holy Spirit nudging you to do something, whether to change a behavior, witness to someone or whatever.

   Describe a time when another Christian communicated an insight that helped you with some situation.

Have you ever read your Bible and a particular verse or story jumped out at you in a way that it hadn't before? What was it?

Can you describe a time in your life that God spoke to you through your circumstances?

4. Sometimes Satan likes to hide behind things that seem really great: a good-looking person, a leadership position, a popular boy asking you out, etc. How can you know the difference between Satan's schemes and God's true voice? Use the following verses to help you answer: 1 Corinthians 2:10-14; 1 John 4:1-6.

5. Knowing God's voice and obeying it are two different things. Have you ever disobeyed when you knew your actions went against God's plan? How did it make you feel when you realized you had passed up an opportunity to obey God? How do you think it made God feel?

Beyond Plastic . . . .

Hearing God's voice can be a tricky thing. You must constantly renew your heart and mind in him so that you have a quiet spirit that is receptive to hearing him. Stop and ask God to prepare your heart to hear the Holy Spirit. Ask him not only to speak to you but to help you be obedient as well. If you're waiting for specific direction from him, God will be faithful!

HOPE TO CARRY ON

We know that suffering produces perseverance; perseverance, character; and character, hope. And hope does not disappoint us, because God has poured out his love into our hearts by the Holy Spirit, whom he has given us.

Romans 5:3-5 (NIV)

One of my favorite movies stars Sandra Bullock and Harry Connick, Jr. I saw it three times at the theater, and now I own the video and watch it at home. Being the hopeful romantic that I am, purchasing chick flicks is often a necessity. In this film, although the boy does win the girl at the very end, it isn't until the last, brief moment before the credits roll that we discover exactly why the film is named *Hope Floats.*

Yet if we look closely throughout the movie, the meaning is implied many times. It is only by leaning on the gift of hope that the film's characters endure and overcome the numerous difficulties they face: spouses having affairs, dying parents, loved ones who are ill, depression and difficult relationships. Sandra Bullock's character says that when things look bad, "You have to give hope a chance to float up to the top."

What is even better than what Birdie Pruitt (Bullock's character) tells us is what God reveals to us in Romans 5:5: "hope does not disappoint us, because God has poured out his love into our hearts by the Holy Spirit, whom he has given us" (NIV). What a gift! I have endured some very difficult circumstances lately. Sometimes these problems look like mountains looming in front of me. What a comfort hope has been to me during these times. Things have not always worked out as I have wanted, but the act of hoping in Christ has never disappointed me. Sometimes hoping for some sort of God-given joy to come on the other side of a difficult circumstance is the only thing that carries me through.

What do you hope for? A certain grade? A certain boy to ask you out? A certain friendship to develop? Physical healing for someone you love? Emotional healing for a relationship you are in? Parents to stop fighting? Acceptance into a certain organization or college? Whatever it is, hope will not disappoint you. Circumstances may fail you, and people most definitely will. But with perseverance comes character and with character comes hope (Romans 5:4). We need to give hope a chance!

Anything But Plastic

. . . .

1. Everyone hopes for things. No hope is silly. What do you hope for at this time in your life?

2. Look up the word *hope* in a dictionary. Define both the noun and verb forms of *hope*.

3. Name some things or people that you have placed your hope in before. Do these things or people always meet your desires and remain faithful to you? How does it make you feel when people let you down?

4. Is there something you have gone through or are still dealing with that has drowned out part of your hope? What keeps you from hoping in Christ?

5. Read the following verses: Job 13:15; Psalm 38:15; Psalm 39:7; Romans 12:12. Do you think the authors of these verses always hoped from within stable circumstances? In whom did these people hope?

6. Read Psalm 71:5. Do you place your hope in God now in the same way you did as a child? Why or why not?

Beyond Plastic . . . .

How does your "hope department" look? Are you placing your confidence in God right now? It couldn't be a better time to hope in God. People and circumstances will disappoint you, but God never will!

AMERICAN iDOLS

Do not make idols of any kind, whether in the shape of birds or animals or fish. You must never worship or bow down to them.

Exodus 20:4, 5

Did you play dress up when you were younger? As a little girl, I loved to play dress up, especially at birthday parties. I would put on old ballet costumes or my mother's clothes. I used to pull out her high heels and the box of gaudy costume jewelry, and on very rare occasions, when my mom was feeling brave, I could wear her makeup or fingernail polish. With my grown-up outfit on, I quickly assumed a new identity for the afternoon. I was an adult. I could have tea parties, go to the store, walk around and toss my hair to reveal my new earrings. My friends and I tried anything to look older. We even put plastic pantyhose eggs in our shirts! I just wanted to be like the big girls.

As I grew up, I still played dress up, but in a different way. In high school,

God placed various people in my life that I looked up to and wanted to pattern myself after. I noticed the way they dressed, the way they wrote, their hobbies, the things that made them laugh. One teacher of mine in particular fascinated me so much that I often just watched her. I wasn't a stalker—I just wanted to see what made her unique and successful. I even remember the insignificant things that made her cool to me.

She wore a gold ring on almost every finger. When she talked to us, she would roll a pencil back and forth between her hands, making a distinctive clicking noise as the pencil bounced across her jewelry. It wasn't that this made her an exciting person—it just made her herself. I decided that when I got older, I wanted to have a ton of rings like hers; in many ways I wanted to be just like her.

For the most part, this fascination that I had with being like my teacher was harmless. I looked up to her, and that challenged me to be a better person, to search for my true identity and to find what I was good at. I never did buy a bunch of gold rings; I don't roll a pencil when I talk. But there are many things that I still do just like her and my other mentors, because I found out those things work! Then again, there are many things my role models did that don't fit me or my personality at all. So I don't imitate those qualities.

People are imitators by nature. We take tips from magazines. We dress according to what the fashion world dictates. And we even get a lot of our verbal expressions and habits from things we've seen in books, television and movies. But we need to be careful, because what we choose to imitate can make or break who we are. When we start to see people as more than role models, when we begin to obsess about being like them in every way, we cross a dangerous boundary. When admiration turns into obsession, we are forced into disobedience to God. When we pay too much attention to being like other people, we stop trying so hard to be like Christ. This behavior creates idols that slowly creep into our hearts and minds and crowd Christ out of them.

Have you ever heard anyone say, "She's my idol"? I hear it all of the time when people talk about famous athletes and movie stars. She's my idol! *Idol?* Role model, inspiration, mentor—maybe! But God makes it clear in his Word that when we create idols we are disobedient. We are not to elevate anyone or anything above him. God gives us mentors and role models, and when we look up to them and learn from them, God will use that to develop our character. But his ultimate desire is for our focus to stay on *him*. Playing dress up is a fun way to spend an afternoon. But God wants us to play dress up every day, modeling ourselves after him. His image will never disappoint us. What a perfect example to imitate!

Anything But Plastic

1. It is important to choose good role models and to learn from them. Name three people that you truly respect. What inner qualities do they possess that you wish to see someday in your life?

2. As much as you look up to your role models, can you see their imperfections as well? Do you think it is important to notice that people have imperfections as well as strengths? Why or why not?

3. It is critical that you don't confuse respect for others with idolizing them. It is important never to allow them to occupy a place in your life that only God can fill. Are you guilty of elevating someone in your life to the level of idolatry? In what ways do you think you do this?

4. Read Ephesians 5:1. What does Paul encourage you to do?

Beyond Plastic. . . . .

Have you chosen Jesus as your best role model? In what areas of your life do you think you are patterning yourself after Christ? Allow him to occupy his rightful place in your heart and watch what happens!

JUST A SEC

As a modern consumer you have been programmed to expect a quick-fix lifestyle. You can get fast food, use express lines, zap your dinner in microwave ovens, buy now and pay later, fax it rather than mail it, text message rather than call. Now! Now! Now! However, in the Christian life, many times you are called upon to wait . . . and wait . . . and wait.

I have read the verse above many times before, but it hit me differently today. I am at a point in my life where I feel like a stranger to myself, sort of as if I am standing on the outside of my life looking in. Do you ever feel like this? As I enter my thirties, life is a bit scarier than I expected, because so far, not much of it is even close to how I had assumed it would be. I planned on getting married right out of college, traveling a bunch, working at a particular school and perhaps having two or three daughters by now. In addition to the fact that none of this has happened, I feel like God may be calling me to do some things for him in my life that I am only now being exposed to.

Why now? Why didn't he reveal these things to me when I graduated from college? Why do I still live where I do? Why haven't I switched jobs in years? Why am I still single? Maybe I should just quit my job and start over. Maybe I should lower my standards for a date. Or maybe the question I should ask myself is . . . why on earth is it so hard for me to wait?

If we were honest, we would admit that there are times when we will wait forever for certain things if we know we're going to get them in the end. What about camping out overnight for tickets to that concert you just have to see? Or standing in the checkout line to pay for that perfect clothing item that your mom is finally willing to buy for you? Or maybe you sit by the phone or computer every evening waiting for that guy you like to just call or "IM" you. Maybe you even waste time in the mile-long drive-thru line for something as simple as a drink (I'm guilty of this one)!

Why then is waiting so difficult, especially when the result of waiting often brings things that are even better than what we originally desired? I know Jesus wants to give you and me what we need and what is the absolute best for us. He wants to give us the desires of our hearts—to give us amazing, abundant lives! He wants to give us something even better than what we are praying and waiting for. The question is, will we let him?

What are you waiting for God to provide for you or to do in your life? Better yet, what are you *not* waiting for very well? Ask God to make the wait worth your while. Ask him to make the holding period a time of growth. Ask him to show you what you can do for him in the meantime, rather than be depressed and complain about what he's *not* doing for you. As the verse says, be courageous and simply wait. Get in line for what God has for you. It is a wait you don't want to miss!

Anything But Plastic

1. Read Isaiah 40:30, 31. What do even young people do in these verses?

   Waiting upon the Lord, according to Isaiah, means placing your faith or confidence in him and giving him the time to act on behalf of your situation. Reflect on your life and list three things that you are waiting for at the present time.

2. What is your attitude toward waiting for each one of these things? Why do you think it can be so difficult to wait for some things?

3. All through Scripture, God makes promises and calls various individuals to accomplish certain tasks. Without a doubt, one of the greatest challenges to each individual was to wait upon God, trusting in him to keep his promises. Name at least three such individuals in the Bible who had to wait for God. How did each one handle the waiting period?

4. See if you can find three reasons God may require you to wait. First read Hebrews 11:6. What does this verse say about faith? Can you name a time when you think it ended up being a good thing that you had to wait for something?

In 1 Samuel 16–31, we see David going through a period of ten excruciatingly difficult years during which God trained him to be the king of Israel. Do you have a sense of something that God may be preparing you to do? What is it? What aspects of your character do you think God is still working on?

In John 11:1–45, we can see that sometimes God may delay answers to prayers in order for us to experience him in a different way or on another level. Have you ever prayed for something that God didn't answer right away? What was it? What did you learn about God in the process?

Beyond Plastic. . . . .

Talk to God about any lack of patience that is currently going on in your life. Admit to him your thoughts and feelings and seek his forgiveness for your impatience. Ask him to enlarge your faith and sustain you as you wait for him!

LEAVE YOUR MARK

"Your brother never gave me trouble."
"She's our oldest—the pretty one."
"Our younger son got the brains."
"She will never amount to much."
"Why can't you be like your sister?"

Statements like these are all too common and painfully familiar to some of us. Maybe your parents or teachers never said anything like this to you, but you saw it written in their eyes or in the expressions on their faces. If you are anything like me, you sometimes feel much less than perfect, perhaps even as if you have failed.

But do you know there is always going to be someone who is prettier than you, smarter than you or who runs a better race than you? And that's OK!

You are who you are because that's who God made you to be. Our heavenly creator is a firm believer in individuality, and he makes no mistakes!

Thinking of individuality reminds me of sugar cookies. My mom had a huge tin can full of cookie cutters shaped like animals, hearts, flowers, holiday objects and even cartoon characters. I used to dig deep until I found the ones I wanted for each batch of cookies. Once I selected the cutters, more jobs followed: rolling out the dough, putting the shapes on a pan and decorating, a chore I took quite seriously!

Sprinkles, candy confetti and beads of various colors all had to be spread out to make each cookie appear unique. But do you know, in all my years of cookie making, I always had at least two cookies that looked the same. No matter how hard I tried to make them different, I eventually got tired or bored and would lazily throw sprinkles here and there, just to get the job done. What started out as an exciting project quickly lost its appeal and I moved on to something else.

Thank goodness that when God formed you and me, he did not use cutters. He does not stamp his children out in mass production and throw a tiny difference on us here and there. There are so many things that can be potentially different about people: hair color, eye color, height, shape, leg length, complexion, temper, sense of humor, talents, intelligence, spiritual gifts—the list goes on. You may find someone with many similarities to you, but you'll never find someone who is *exactly* like you.

God never gets tired and lazy when he works on his children; he took several measures to make sure that you are never confused with anyone else. God gave you a certain set of dental records that are unmatchable. He gave you a fingerprint that is uniquely yours. And almost everyone possesses a birthmark that is an original. I have one that is shaped like a heart, which I use as a reminder of God's love for me. God marks you as his own creation in many different ways.

It doesn't matter if your sibling or friend has a talent you don't. Or if you don't really resemble the "hims" or "hers" of your life that seem to have it more together than you do. The more you and I try to imitate others, the more we stray from being the unique people our Father so purposefully designed us to be!

God reminds his children of this very gift of individuality in Isaiah 49:16. The words here say our names are inscribed on God's palm, and I like to think that he actually holds us so tightly, we leave a mark on him. Have you ever fallen asleep on a blanket or a sweater, only to wake up and find the imprint of the fabric's pattern on your skin? Because God holds us safely, there is an original you and me etched into God's hand. No two of us are alike! And he made us individuals so that we can leave a mark on those around us.

Are you sadly scurrying about, attempting to be like someone else? Or are you happily and victoriously succeeding in being an original and unique, God-made *you*? Don't be afraid to be yourself! Deep down, despite what they may say, people will admire you for it, and God will be proud of you. Being different is one of the reasons he made you. When times get tough and you forget who you are, just turn to the Father. Ask him to show you your mark on his hand.

Anything But Plastic

. . . .

1. Think really hard for a few moments about the traits you possess that make you uniquely *you*! Even if those traits may annoy others, what makes you yourself?

2. Can you think of a time when God used you precisely through these very unique traits that he gave you? Describe this time.

3. What, on the other hand, are one or two of the habits that perhaps you have lazily settled into that need to be worked on? Why do you think God made you like this if he wanted you to change these things?

Read Philippians 1:6; Hebrews 12:1, 2. Write some reasons God desires to bring about change in your life.

4. My favorite definition that I found of the word *inscribe* is "to fix or impress deeply or lastingly in the mind." How does it make you feel to know that God has fixed you lastingly on his palm and in his heart and mind?

5. Do you think it is wrong to want to be like someone else? Explain your answer.

Name a couple of people in your life that you admire. What specific traits do you see in their characters that you desire in order to resemble Christ more?

Beyond Plastic . . . .

Take a look again at Isaiah 49:16. You might want to write it down and carry it with you. It can be a great daily reminder of the "you" God created specially and uniquely!

GREEN'S NOT YOUR BEST COLOR

Do not envy others—it only leads to harm.

Psalm 37:8

"Does this color look good on me?"

"You're an autumn, right? I bet you look so good in brown!"

"My power color is black!"

"What's your best color?"

All of this talk of colors is fairly common among females. Let's face it—girls love color! To be fashionable you usually have to know what it takes to be the best you. But I've got a question. How do you look in green? Yeah, that's right—green!

Green is one of my all-time favorite colors. I love green—all shades of it! So I guess it figures that God would use my love for green to teach me some serious lessons. I'm not sure which author first used the color green as a symbol for envy

in literature. I'm going with Shakespeare. But I can tell you that the green-eyed monster was at the root of many struggles in my Christian walk throughout my teenage years.

The way I see it, there are two ways that envy affects a person's life: you are either the target of someone's envy or you are the very embodiment of envy yourself. For me, being the target is the worst! All of my Christian life, I have desired to be the lady that God asks of me. I strive to exhibit Christlike qualities in my character, in my personality, in my relationships and in my walk with him. Even as a teenager, I wanted to have integrity in my friendships, my goal-setting and in taking care of the physical appearance that God gave me.

My quest for integrity and purity was a personal goal. I was in no way attempting to show off or to be stuck up. I just did it because Christ asks it of us. But there were times I ended up in tears because my friends ignored me and talked about me behind my back—or even right in front of my face, for that matter. I never figured out why my desire to work hard and mind my own business colored my friends an ugly shade of green. But the meanness and envy that oozed forth from girls when I was younger is still alive and kicking in teenagers today.

The way I figure it, sometimes we look down on people in an effort to feel better about ourselves. There is a human tendency to be threatened by people who are really beautiful or who have tons of friends. We envy those who possess a trait that we desire, such as humor, intelligence or kindness. We tend to resent those who have a skill we admire but are terrible at ourselves. We often see successful people as a threat, and we feel worse about ourselves in the process.

That means that instead of appreciating these incredible qualities in other people, we become envious of them and shut them out. I see this happening time after time to some of my nicest students. As they go along, minding their own business—wham!—out of nowhere they make the teenage hit list of people to snub for the day. Dishing out this kind of hostility is an unattractive and damaging activity.

Truthfully, I'm plagued with this bug too. That's right. I still turn a nice shade of green every now and then. Sometimes I think the older I get, the *worse* it gets! When I look at my life, I am at a big crossroads where nothing is what I predicted! My job is not what I assumed it would be. I still struggle with being over thirty and single. Every time someone flashes an engagement ring in my face, a tinge of envy shoots through my veins!

God calls Christians to be better than that, and he deals with me every time my heart chooses envy. He has to constantly remind me that his plan for me is not the same as his plan for anyone else. He gives each one of us different appearances, different spiritual gifts, different talents and even different weaknesses, because he wants each of his children to be unique. I have to remember that what God has planned for the people I'm envious of are not the same things he has planned for me. And his timing for me is not his timing for you.

Thank goodness he's still in charge of the color palate. Envy isn't the only quality symbolized with green. Green also represents growth and newness! When trees and yards sprout again after a long winter, what color are they just bursting with? Green of course! What if, every time we feel envy creeping in, we recognize that God has a lesson to teach as well? He can use those opportunities as a time to renew our mindset, to redirect us and to provide us with a fresh start to grow in his work. What if he is sprinkling a little shower of renewal on us as a reminder that he is not finished with us?

Growing up, one of my must-see TV shows was *The Muppet Show*. Good ol' Kermie used to say, "It's not easy being green." As a frog, Kermit probably just meant that looking different from everyone else was tough. But maybe God wants us to *be* green. Not green with envy, but green with newness and growth. He puts challenges in our paths to give us opportunities to grow. So when that challenge arrives to test you, like seeing that pretty girl get asked out by the hot guy, you could respond with resentment or you can allow freshness to rain down on you. Which color of green will you be? It's not easy being green, but it might be your best color when you wear it the right way!

Anything But Plastic

1. People don't like to admit they struggle with envy. But most of us would be lying if we said it wasn't a problem. Who are some people that you envy?

2. Why do you think girls get envious of others?

   Read Exodus 20:17. Do any of these things look like the answers you just gave? Which ones?

3. Why do you think we covet what others possess? Would you say that you are a needy person? Do you think you have a right to want what others have?

   Read the following verses. Make a note regarding what each verse says about envy or jealousy.

   Galatians 5:26:

   1 Peter 2:1:

4. What are you like when you envy others? According to the following verses, what would a Christlike response to envy be?

Philippians 4:11:

1 Timothy 6:8:

5. We often use envy and jealousy to mean the same thing, but to be jealous mainly means to be "intolerant of rivalry or unfaithfulness." Exodus 20:5 says that God is a jealous God. Why is God jealous?

God wants us for his own, and he wants to give us all we need. Read Psalm 23. From this psalm, why should you be content?

Beyond Plastic. . . . .

Wouldn't it be better to have a contented soul rather than an envious heart? If envy is a problem for you, stop and pray right now that God would be in control of your "greenness," that he would produce growth and newness in your character and in your heart. It's God's green or Satan's green. Whose color will you wear today?

HAPPY BIRTHDAY TO WHO?

*The Savior—yes, the Messiah, the Lord—
has been born tonight in Bethlehem, the city of David!*

Luke 2:11

Christmastime was always magical for me as a little girl. I can remember writing a letter to Santa Claus every year and mailing it. I eagerly waited to go to the mall to have my picture taken with him and to reinforce my wish list. I recall the magic in Christmas coloring books—I took such pride in making the pictures come to life. I can still almost taste the freshly baked sugar cookies that I so delicately decorated with colored sprinkles, icing and silver beads. Can't you almost feel Christmas?

Every year I couldn't wait to put on my Nutcracker costume and capture my shining moment on stage. *Everybody—look at me! Watch me dance!* I set out luminarias on our street and put wooden Christmas characters up to make my yard sparkle like a fairyland. I woke up on Christmas morning, jumped from my bed and ran to the tree to find an undeserved number of gifts—just for me. I truly wanted for nothing. Christmastime was all about excitement, and when I was a child, Christmas was usually all about *me*.

I never intended for it to be a selfish thing. I don't really think anyone starts the holiday season and says, "How can I make this Christmas all about me? What all can I do for myself this year? How can I receive the most gifts possible and consume all of my family's time during this Christmas season?"

But ever so sneakily, our focus shifts from the one true meaning of the whole season. For a lot of Christians, Christmas becomes a selfish time. Our actions, our wish lists, our shopping desires all seem to sing out, "Happy Birthday to *me!*"

Yet over 2,000 years ago in a dark stable, a young mother shivered in the cold. She had ridden for days on a donkey (probably), endured a pre-epidural delivery, and rented an unheated room. But her thoughts were about anything *but* herself. Instead, as she cradled the Savior of the world in her arms and rocked him to sleep, I can only imagine the sweet sound of her lullabies or the softness in her voice as she whispered happy birthday to her son, Jesus. There was nothing about Mary's Christmas that screamed, "Look at me!"

What an awesome day Christ's birthday is for all of us. God did give us a gift the day he sent his Son into the world. On that day, he provided us with a present that we should treasure more than any sweater, any music player or even any car parked in the driveway. In a simple manger, surrounded by his selfless parents, Jesus Christ, the most perfect provision for our salvation, peace and joy, quietly entered this world.

Thousands of years later, what tune are you rocking to during the month of December? Do you sing "Happy Birthday to Me"? Or does your life celebrate Jesus' birthday? He is truly the honored guest of the party. Yet unlike us, Jesus does not ask for material gifts or possessions. He doesn't mail us a wish list of all of the goods he hopes to receive. He simply asks us for ourselves—our wholehearted love, devotion and worship.

What gifts do you have to offer him this season? What are your talents? Can you bake, sing, play an instrument or dance? Can you spread joy to someone through those gifts? Can you help someone less fortunate than you find joy in the holiday season? Do you have extra time to offer? Or maybe you have a friendly smile?

Can you give Christ your service in a less visual way? Are you a prayer warrior? Pray for those less fortunate than you. Are you an encourager? People often get depressed during the holidays. Sometimes people are lonely. Maybe you could write notes to tell them why they are special and remind them of God's love. Are you blessed with extra finances that will allow you to make someone else's Christmas more special?

God asks for treasures of the heart. I promise you that when you start singing "Happy Birthday" to him through your actions, your heart will follow, and Christmas will take on a different meaning for you. Sing loudly to him, for you have great reason to celebrate. A Savior has been born for you!

Anything But Plastic

1. Have you ever been guilty of singing "Happy Birthday to Me" with your actions—not just at Christmastime, but on a day-to-day basis?

2. As a child, what were your family Christmas traditions that catered specifically to you and to your enjoyment?

   Did you have any traditions that acknowledged that it was Jesus' birthday, rather than just a greeting-card holiday? If not, can you think of some Christ-centered traditions that you might like to start now or for your own children someday?

3. It is often more fun to be the gift-giver than the gift-getter. There is an ultimate gift-giver we need to recognize in our lives. Read Romans 5:15-17. What was the gift Jesus gave us? To whom is that gift available?

   In Romans 6:23, you see another reference to a gift from God. What adjective does your Bible use to describe the gift?

4. Christians have many gifts in their lives; often they have so many that they don't even recognize them as gifts. Take a moment to list some gifts you have that fit into categories such as material gifts, talents, spiritual gifts or relational gifts.

Read James 1:17. How does this verse describe gifts from God? How does the verse describe the gift-giver? Do you think God knows what he is doing when he gives us things?

5. We've read a lot about receiving gifts, but how good are you at giving them?

Read Acts 20:35. What does this verse say about giving?

Read 2 Corinthians 9:7. What type of attitude does God want you to have when you give?

Look back at your list in question four and write one way that you are a *giver* in each of those categories.

Beyond Plastic . . . .

I am sure if we tried, we could all be better givers than we are right now. What is something you could really be excited about giving and sharing with others? Remember, God loves a cheerful giver!

GOT JOY?

Have you ever seen people who just *look* unhappy? You can see it in their eyes, the look on their faces or the droop of their shoulders—they believe their world is falling apart. I read in a book recently that happiness is a result of the circumstances around you, but joy is created *in spite* of the circumstances around you. When the circumstances around you are bad, do you sulk, yell or slam doors in anger? Or in spite of the negative events you encounter, do you react with joy?

Everyone will have some disappointment in life. We cannot possibly be expected to live life without ever being upset by the sad or negative things that happen to us and to our loved ones. But as a Christian, I am continually reminded to step up to a higher level when I am disappointed. Instead of wallowing in unhappiness, I am called to seek an attitude of joy. Being joyful does not require me to go around with a phony laugh and cheesy smile on my face even though my heart might be breaking on the inside. Joy should be a reflection of my character (what is on the inside) as opposed to my circumstances (what is on the outside).

When Jesus faced the cross, the Bible says he did it because of the joy that would be his afterward (Hebrews 12:2). He did not want to do it. He even asked his Father in Heaven if there was any other way to take care of matters. But the benefit that his death on the cross gave to others far outweighed any physical suffering or unhappiness it caused him.

I am a person who naturally has a serious expression on my face. Because I often appear to be deep in thought, focused, and perhaps am not always smiling, people sometimes ask me what's wrong. I may not always show happiness, but I do hope and pray that God will cause my character to reflect *joy*—the joy that will seep out from the inside so that others will have no doubt as to how I survive difficult circumstances. Happiness and joy do not always go hand in hand.

Happiness will not get us through the hard times, but joy will.

How do others see you when things do not always go well in your life? Do they see the bitter outside or do you shine through with a radiant and joyful character? Pray with me that we will use our trials to allow others to see God in us. The world around us may bring us down, but God can make us joyful if we let him. The choice is ours. The world's circumstances might cause some happiness. But God's circumstances produce joy!

Anything But Plastic

. . . .

1. God provides both happiness and joy. What things have happened in your life that made you absolutely happy?

2. People in the Bible proclaimed their happiness too. Read Genesis 30:9-13. Why was Leah happy?

Happiness is a great response. But is happiness able to carry you through bad circumstances? How do you think Leah's happiness would have changed if something bad, such as a kidnapping, had happened to her baby?

3. In many situations in my life, I have lost all or almost all of my happiness. What circumstances have happened to you that have taken away your happiness? Be specific.

4. What do you think the solution is to this happiness-robbery? When happiness is missing, with what Christlike quality does God want to replace it?

Read 1 Peter 1:5-8. Why can you be glad even though you endure trials?

God knows that you need help from him. Psalm 51:12 is a great verse to pray when you feel like you've lost your joy. In this verse what does David ask God to do?

Beyond Plastic . . . .

You can have happiness temporarily, but it may disappear after the happy event is over. If there is no joy in your life at that time, you'll be left with an empty void. But if a godly joy is present at all times, you can always be content, even when the world doesn't hand you anything to be happy about. Ask God to provide you with joy when you see a happiness-robbing moment sneaking into your life. Happiness is from God too, but his joy is insurmountable!

DON'T READ THE LABEL

But the Lord said to Samuel, ". . . The Lord doesn't make decisions the way you do! People judge by outward appearance, but the Lord looks at a person's thoughts and intentions."

1 Samuel 16:7

If I could get paid for people-watching, I would *so* be rich. Mannerisms, facial expressions, eye contact, hand gestures and the way people talk, walk, dress and flirt—these little intricacies of human behavior fascinate me. But I have found that I must be very careful with my hobby. I've never considered myself a prejudiced person as far as race is concerned, but I admit that at times I struggle with prejudging people in a very different way.

In my opinion, being prejudiced is making assumptions about what a person is like based on a first glance or existing stereotypes. Most of us are guilty of this at some point or another. In Joshua 2, a woman named Rahab plays an integral part in helping the Israelites conquer the land of Canaan. This woman was guilty of one of the very sins among the Canaanites that disgusted God. Yet in spite of her prostitute job and her lying tongue, Rahab still had the faith to believe God could deliver her and her family. And he did. Because she helped Joshua's spies escape from the city's soldiers, God faithfully delivered the land of Canaan into the Israelites' hands, and the Israelites spared Rahab's life.

The Israelites could have said, "Ain't no way I'm hidin' out in a prostitute's house. You can't trust 'em." But instead they trusted her with their lives. God could have looked at Rahab and said, "This woman is dirty and rough—simply not an acceptable tool for me to use to carry out my plan." But God chose instead to make Rahab a part of the genealogy of Jesus the Messiah! She became one of the key Bible characters in the fourteen generations of chosen people who were Christ's ancestors.

As I said, I struggle with my own prejudices. Where I teach, kids tend to get labeled: preps, skaters, punks, jocks, kickers, etc. It is so easy to have preconceived ideas about people just because they dress a certain way. I used to be guilty of labeling. When a multiple-pierced, maroon-haired student wearing baggy, bell-bottomed pants and a long untucked shirt walked into my classroom at the start of the term, I'd think, *Oh, God, help me. This is going to be a long semester!*

But I'd learn that I was wrong! Some of the nicest kids I've ever taught fall into these baggy-pants-wearing, dyed-hair, studded-tongue categories. In fact, one of my punk boys turned out to be the sweetest, most well-mannered, caring guy in the class. He even made the effort to say "Bless you" whenever anyone sneezed! I had to laugh out loud when I saw him one summer at a video store wearing khaki shorts and tennis shoes and looking just as straight-laced as could be. But even before that, his baggy clothing did not change the fact that this was an awesome kid. Neither does a person's race, religion, shape, clothing or hair color determine who that person is. God does not play favorites and he does not judge by the outward appearance. Maybe it's time we actually clued in—we might be missing out on getting to know someone totally cool!

Anything But Plastic

1. The world is a scary place to live today, and sometimes we don't know who to trust. Many times, however, our prejudices don't come from legitimate fear but from preconceived ideas. Can you name some people that you judged wrongly just because of their personal appearance? List what it was that made you place judgment on each person.

2. Should we *never* pay attention to the way people look? Why or why not? What does an employer look for when a candidate comes in for a job interview? List several characteristics.

   What are some aspects about the appearance or behavior of others that you think God would *want* you to be aware of?

3. Read Acts 8:26-37. Given the Ethiopian's job description, how do you think he might have been dressed?

In verses 30 and 31, does Philip hesitate or think twice about approaching this stranger?

Philip does not judge the Ethiopian by his skin color, job description or anything else. Because of Philip's obedience to the Spirit's instructions, what happens to the Ethiopian?

4. Read Matthew 7:1, 2. What does Jesus warn you about?

Beyond Plastic

Don't base your opinion of someone on just a glance. Take some time to look closer—you never know what cool person you might see there. Don't forget—the Lord looks at the heart!

MORE THAN A WOMAN

Charm is deceptive, and beauty does not last;
but a woman who fears the Lord will be greatly praised.

Proverbs 31:30

I still remember an encounter I had on a family vacation when I was only about eight years old. We had stopped at a gas station, and while I was in the bathroom, a woman suddenly pounded on my stall door, barking in a deep voice for me to hurry up. She startled me so badly that I almost cried. When I finally opened the door and headed back out to the car, she said something like, "Well, it's about time!" My mom, fully aware that something had flustered me, asked me to rehash the trauma. I ended my story by saying, "That lady was really rude to me!"

My mom then said something to me that I never forgot. She told me, "Mieka, that was no lady, that was a woman."

Any female human being can be a woman, but it takes something more to be a lady. As I approached my teenage years, my mom bought me a book entitled *Miss Manners*. In it, I found a wealth of information on how to conduct myself as a lady. It included tips for proper table etiquette, proper conversation to match the setting, proper dress for different occasions, how to introduce people, how to communicate through writing or speech and how to behave as a guest in someone's home. I learned a great deal from this book, as well as from my mom's example.

I feel very strongly about being a lady. In working with teen girls, it has always been my desire to pass those values on to them. It upsets me when I see girls today being what I know is less than what God made them to be. Now, I'm not implying that being a lady means life's no fun—it does not require that you sit around all day looking pretty, talking about boring things with your nose in the air and your pinkie pointing away from your cup of tea. You don't have to eliminate laughter, giddiness and excitement from your life. But you should take a closer look at your actions and the effect they have on those around you.

Even though I learned a lot from that book Mom bought for me, her lifestyle has directed me toward an even better source of information: the Bible, and specifically, Proverbs 31.

I believe God desires us to resemble ladies in our actions and treatment of others, our carriage and disposition and our walk with him. Though Proverbs 31 speaks about a virtuous wife, it is full of characteristics of any true lady, whether married or single: she is productive, caring, creative, frugal, hardworking, generous, protective and energetic. A lady exhibits these qualities through her treatment of others. She is not selfish; rather, she always looks first to the needs of those around her. She pays attention to the words of her mouth, knowing full well that gossiping, cussing and saying mean things about people could be a hindrance to others.

Notice—not one of these things has to do with what this woman looks like or what the guys think about her. But God wants us to be ladylike in our physical demeanor as well. This one really gets to me. Our society today, particularly the fashion industry, is pushing girls further and further away from looking like ladies. The skirts get shorter and the necklines get lower. As a teacher, I see more cleavage, stomachs and thongs than I would dare to count—even on sweet, Christian girls. Everyone wants to be in style, because the girls in the magazines and videos wear things "that way."

Don't get me wrong, I love being fashionable and stylish with my clothes! But what I love even more is that God encourages me to be a little different from the rest of the world. I like being different so much that if everyone else is wearing something, particularly the girls in the videos, then I don't want any part of it! In following God's call to be a lady, I try to act, dress and carry myself in a manner that doesn't reveal everything I've got to the guys around me. It is hard when I see men running after other girls in skimpier styles. But I like to think that men *might* find me a bit mysterious or even better, Christlike. And who wants a guy who falls for such obvious bait anyway?

Besides, though you may not realize it, your appearance can be a *huge* stumbling block to guys of all ages around you. Not only are girls wearing more revealing clothes, but many young women are also forgetting how to sit and behave appropriately. In my drill team study hall, I have seen way too many flashes of underwear and derrieres as girls plop down in their chairs or bend over to pick something up. Sure, the class is all girls, but it would be so easy for one of them to forget sometime and accidentally do the same thing in front of guys. Where is the mystery, girls? A guy has a difficult enough time controlling his hormones without you adding another coal to the fire! A lady strives to keep from being a temptation to others.

Most important, God desires to develop your ladylike qualities in your walk with him. Are you basing your femininity on what the world wants or on what God asks? You can look to Scripture for details about the character traits God wants us all to have: the kind of speech, thoughts and treatment of others that will separate the men from the gentlemen and the women from the ladies. Even Webster knows the difference.

woman: the female human being, as distinguished from man

lady: a woman who is polite, refined and well-mannered

God longs to do great things in and through your life. But you've got to not let your manners or worldly style get in his way. Let him refine you. Ask him to make you a lady of mystery. He can give you so much more femininity and elegance than any clothes or makeup can! Maybe someday someone will even say about you, "There are many virtuous and capable women in the world, but you surpass them all!" (Proverbs 31:29).

Anything But Plastic

1. If you could pick one person in your life that most resembles a lady, who would you choose? Name three or four things about her that you think make her a lady. Do you see traits in your life that are already starting to resemble those of a Christlike lady? What are those traits?

2. Do you know girls who are less than mysterious—who do *whatever* it takes to get a guy to like them? How does that make you feel?

Maybe you are that girl. Why do you feel you have to look or act the way you do?

3. Describe below, in detail, what you think would be the perfect outfit. What would you wear from head to toe that would make you feel like a lady—attractive and eye-catching in a ladylike way?

4. In each of the Scriptures below, you will discover a part of a godly outfit. Name what that part is and where on your body God asks you to wear these things.

Proverbs 1:8, 9:

Proverbs 3:3:

Proverbs 4:8, 9:

Proverbs 6:20, 21:

Proverbs 7:2, 3:

5. When you have a chance, read Proverbs 31:10–31. Write down here some ladylike qualities that you want to have in your life.

Beyond Plastic. . . . .

After reading Proverbs 31, it may seem like it would almost be easier to wear sleazy clothes and let it all hang out. But it definitely isn't easy to clean up a stained reputation. What will your deeds publicly say about you? Becoming a lady can start with something as simple as picking out a new outfit. Read verses 29–31 again. The reward is worth the trouble!

ON IDLE

*We hear that some of you are living idle lives,
refusing to work and wasting time meddling in other people's business. . . .
Settle down and get to work. . . . never get tired of doing good.*

2 Thessalonians 3:11-13

"Don't be a Lazy Brownie!"

OK, I know, it's kind of cheesy, but this is a phrase that stuck with me throughout my upbringing. Every Christmas my dad read a book entitled *Jolly Old Santa Claus* to my sister and me. Since it was published in 1969, I imagine you are too young to know the story! It takes place in Santa's North Pole workshop. In this tale, Santa refers to all of his elves as "little brownies." The brownies help make the toys and ornaments, bake cookies, sift through letters, keep a list of good boys and girls, care for the reindeer, load the sleigh, await Santa's return and finally, clean up the workshop. What hard workers the "little brownies" are—all except for one: Lazy Brownie!

Lazy Brownie is specifically referred to four times in this twenty-page children's story. The first time, the author says, "Lazy Brownie is always playing! Just look at him riding the rock-a-bye pony when he should be helping." The second reference to our elf friend tells us that Lazy Brownie is still not working yet! He was hiding up on a high shelf. The third time we hear about Lazy B. he is hiding under Santa's desk, smoking a pipe. The narrator tells us, "He's always getting into mischief!"

The last instance of this brownie's laziness is when he is busted visiting with the reindeer while everyone else is working so hard. Lazy Brownie is a perfect example of an idle life. He possesses very little discipline. He always plays when he should be working, hides in the background, gets into mischief and talks at times he shouldn't.

Chances are you have probably been guilty of laziness yourself or you have been stuck with the consequences of someone else's idle ways. Contrary to what some parents might think, hard work *is* often required from teenagers: at this age, many of you hold your first job; you receive group projects in school that require major participation; you strive toward achievements in extracurricular activities, academics, hobbies or talents; and you're working toward entering college. Although your individual endeavors affect you greatly, they affect others around you too—especially when you slack off.

As a teacher, I've seen many students' grades affected by a group member who just sits back and allows the rest of the students to carry the load. I've seen team members be lazy in learning the details of their sport's drills, choosing instead to goof off during practice and causing a weak performance that reflects negatively on the team. I've also watched teenagers working at the mall. Some are really focused, but others spend their hours talking on the phone, chatting with friends and behaving in a less than professional manner. This behavior irritates customers, including me, and often gives the store a bad image.

Besides letting down others, including God, there are also two main ways that our laziness affects us personally. The first way is that it lessens our effectiveness with other people. As Christians, we are called to lead a disciplined life and to be on the ball, because we never know when others are watching us. I would hate for laziness on my part to cause people to think I am not walking with Christ. I would also dread for someone to see me as undependable or too irresponsible to carry out a task.

The other problem with laziness, and Lazy Brownie could tell you from experience, is that it often gets you into mischief. You may think, *Well I'm not a bad person; I won't do anything wrong.* But living an undisciplined life can keep you from being challenged. When you do not channel your thoughts and energies into positive activities, your mind is free to wander into all sorts of thoughts and temptations. Often when the mind wanders, the body follows right behind, putting those thoughts into actions.

This is not to say that God never intends for you to rest or to have a free mind so you are ready for him to speak to you. He does desire you to have quiet and peaceful times. But he has called us to be disciplined, and with that discipline comes the command to "Settle down and get to work." Just live in such a way that no one can ever possibly call *you* "Lazy Brownie."

Anything But Plastic

1. In your own words, how would you define laziness? Is laziness a problem in your life?

2. Do you recall a time when someone did not do a fair share of work on a school project? How about someone who slacked off in a team activity? What happened as a result of this laziness? How did these attitudes or lack of action make you feel?

3. Would you like to be called Lazy Brownie? How do you think people would treat you if they saw you as lazy?

4. Read Proverbs 6:6-11 about the ant who works today to provide for its future. When a lazy person does not follow through with a task or makes excuses about it, what happens?

5. Describe some times when you have been lazy and made excuses. How do you think your laziness made others feel? How has your laziness affected your success in things you have worked for?

Beyond Plastic . . . .

Think of some work you have been putting off and make a plan to do it this week. Strive to be less like Lazy Brownie and more like the hardworking ant, working at the tasks God has given you and pushing on toward your goals and dreams!

MY ULTIMATE VALENTINE

Watching other people receive flowers, chocolate and jewelry—yep, Valentine's Day is one of my all-time favorite days of the year! Maybe I *am* being a bit sarcastic. I really don't care much for Valentine's Day—*at all*! I want to gag when people start talking about their restaurant reservations and their special evenings out on the town, while I go home to sit and watch reruns of '80s flicks and open my gift from Mom and Dad. Not that I don't appreciate my parents' love for me on Valentine's Day. I do, but you know—it's not quite the same!

I finally have come to the conclusion that Valentine's Day is highly overrated. Do we really need a holiday in order to let people know that they are special to us or that we love them? I hope not!

This year, on the eve of the dreaded day, I decided not to annoy others with woe-is-me comments about the lack of male presence in my life. Since I know that God loves me more than any human being is capable, I also decided I'd try to allow God to be my ultimate valentine. Sounds a little weird, maybe, but it actually worked!

For as long as I can remember, one of the things that has gone hand-in-hand with Valentine's Day is the pink box of pastel candy hearts that have messages stamped on them. I think they kind of taste like chalk. But on a whim, I opened a box of those hearts and chose to read the messages with a different attitude than I usually do. Reminded of my attitude makeover, I read the hearts as if the messages were written specially from *God*, my true valentine, to me! The feeling I received from my "heavenly" messages overwhelmed me. Here are some of the many things that I heard God saying to me that day:

Be Mine
Love You
My Way
True Love
Real Love
My Babe
All Mine
My Girl
I Hope

As strange as it seems, these very words on my candy hearts are chiseled into my spiritual heart as well. God's Word promises me this ultimate, never-ending, unconditional love that I tend to seek from a guy. God desires for me to be his—*all his*—and to allow myself to be completely loved by him. What a perfect valentine date!

Does this mean that I will never experience loneliness again or that I no longer yearn for a romantic relationship? Of course it doesn't. But it does give me some perspective on the awesome love that is available to me at this very moment that is far greater than the love any guy can offer.

Do you gripe about your fate and call yourself a loser on Valentine's Day? Let's rethink that one. We are anything but losers! Flowers die, chocolates spoil and sometimes Valentine's Day dinners go straight to the hips, but God's love remains forever. Maybe you should keep a box of candy hearts handy all year round as a reminder of the love God has lavished on you!

Anything But Plastic

1. When you dream of falling in love, what do you hope will happen in your relationship? What are some of the things that you want your dream guy to say to you and do for you to demonstrate his love?

   What parts of your character and your heart do you hope to share with your man that will demonstrate your love for him?

   Consider the people in your life, such as your parents, friends, etc. How do you show them that you love them?

2. We know deep down that no guy will ever compare to God, and nothing will ever compare to the love of God. Read the following verses. For each verse, briefly give a phrase that describes how we should know God loves us.

   Romans 5:5, 8:

   1 John 3:16:

   1 John 4:19:

   As you are reminded of your sinful nature in these verses, how does God's sacrifice and love for you make you feel?

3. Read each of the following verses and write a description of what God expects from you as his child.

Deuteronomy 6:5:

Deuteronomy 10:12, 13:

John 14:23:

John 15:12:

Wow! A lot is expected from you in return for the love God has given you. But read 1 John 4:19 again. How can you be capable of loving?

4. Read 1 Corinthians 13:4–7. List what love is or isn't. It's a pretty intimidating list! Choose three aspects of love that you feel are your strengths and three that you feel you might be lacking in.

Love is hard work! What aspects of love do you most desire for God to show you right now?

Beyond Plastic . . . .

Whether you're going to be sitting at home on the next Valentine's Day or out on the town, pray with me that God will help us love and see love in a way that glorifies him purely.

PICK A SIDE, ANY SIDE!

If you just listen and don't obey, it is like looking at your face in a mirror but doing nothing to improve your appearance. . . . If you claim to be religious but don't control your tongue, you are just fooling yourself, and your religion is worthless.

James 1:23, 26

All right all of you fence-riders! *What? Who, me?*

Maybe that label does not apply to you. You are capable of making a decision and sticking with that decision; you can take a side and support that side. Maybe fence-riding really doesn't describe you, but how about *lukewarm*—neither hot nor cold, neither here nor there? Now think of that expression in terms of your relationship with Christ. Does the label stick?

It embarrasses and shames me to think of the many days when I could be called a fence-rider. I am so guilty of throwing one foot over the fence closer to God, and refusing to release the other foot from my selfish ways. People are so busy, and with that busyness comes self-absorption. We forget about Christ and all of the ministry opportunities he has placed around us. The amount of time we devote to *our* wants, *our* needs and *our* selfish desires amazes me.

We can eat and snack all day as we watch television, but we find it difficult to eat of the fruit of the Spirit. Where are love, joy, peace, patience and the other spiritual nutrients that should be evident in a Christian's life? We can wallow and swim in misery, so often feeling sorry for ourselves, but where is our compassion for others? We can say "Jesus loves you," or "I'll be praying for you," but as soon as our heels hit the church parking lot, "Did you see what she was wearing?"

comes spilling from our mouths. Where are the words that encourage and edify others?

The Bible says that the person who listens to God's Word with good intentions but does not obey is a fence-rider—lukewarm, wishy-washy. It also says that behaving in this manner is similar to looking at yourself in the mirror and then turning around and immediately forgetting what you look like. Sounds impossible, right? But as a Christian, when you live in disobedience you can forget who you are—truly a child of God with a plan and a purpose in life.

I evaluate my walk with Christ often, to check my status as a person who is hot or cold, or perhaps a fence-rider. But I also struggle with accepting myself and the circumstances God has given me. Perhaps if I spent a little more time working on this, I would feel more confident in jumping over to the hot side of the fence where my heart wants to be.

You can't be a listener and then not a doer; you can't be a doer and not a listener. If you spend time working on your internal condition as well as your external image, your entire being will be grounded in Christ. Then you could look in the mirror, turn from it and know exactly who you are. No struggle you come up against, no temptation to gossip, no insult that someone hurls your way will make you flinch in your efforts to be like Christ.

Look into your heart's mirror. Whose reflection do you see? Yours or God's? Think about what you're reflecting as you go throughout the day. Allow him to help you be an effective doer of his Word, and not a forgetful hearer, so that others will know which side of the fence you are on!

Anything But Plastic

1. Give a brief description of what it means to you to be a fence-rider. Be specific. When have you been guilty of riding the fence in your walk with Christ?

2. Read Revelation 3:15, 16. These verses deal with the way Jesus views his lukewarm children. What does Christ say he would rather they be? What will he do to his lukewarm servants?

3. Lukewarm followers of Christ will look in a "mirror" (God's Word) and go away, forgetting the very identity they have in Christ. Think about the image you reflect to others. What do you think it's like? How much do you reflect Christ?

4. If your reflection is not even close to being like Christ, what do you think is missing from the picture? Read Galatians 5:22, 23. Which fruit of the Spirit needs to do some growing in your life?

Beyond Plastic

God is calling you down from your fence. Ask him to help you stand boldly on his side. The closer you get to him, the easier it will be to reflect him to those around you. Before you know it, you'll be hot!

CAUGHT IN THE COOKIE JAR

There are six things the Lord hates—no, seven things he detests: haughty eyes, a lying tongue, hands that kill the innocent, a heart that plots evil, feet that race to do wrong, a false witness who pours out lies, a person who sows discord among brothers.

Proverbs 6:16-19

Mom (suspicious): "Mieka, have you been to the Cookie Lady's house?"
Little Me (wearing chocolate crumbs on my face): "No ma'am."

So busted!

Living nearby my childhood home was an elderly woman who the neighborhood kids dubbed "the Cookie Lady." When we visited her daily and asked politely, she would hand out cookies. It was a great system, really—she had company every day and I was able to satisfy my sweet tooth.

But one evening, I had specific instructions from my mom to stay away from the Cookie Lady's house, because "dessert will spoil your dinner" (you know the routine). So I went outside to play. A while later I went back inside and, well—you know the rest of the story.

I have to say here that I was mostly a pretty good kid. But the times I did get in trouble always involved my disobedient mouth! In Proverbs 6, God lists seven things that he detests. Since lying is on that list *twice,* I figure maybe God felt the need to place an emphasis on the deceitful tongue just for me.

You'd think that I would have learned a lesson from the Cookie Lady episode, but that wasn't the last time I got caught in a lie. There was once a loose strip of wallpaper hanging down by our toilet. As I sat there one day, in a moment of temporary insanity, I reached over and yanked the paper off. As the ripping sound echoed through the bathroom, my parents' words suddenly came back to me: "Girls, please don't mess with the wallpaper in the bathroom until we can get around to fixing it."

So what was my response to the question, "Mieka, did you tear off the wallpaper?"

"Uh—no," I said, knowing full well that my parents really knew the truth.

As dense as I was, it was because of this very problem with lying that I became a Christian. As a first grader, I asked my mom one day if I could take my gum to school. Of course she answered no, and sent me to the bus stop. Imagine how I felt when only minutes later my sweet and loving mother arrived at the bus stop, bringing the napkin that she had "accidentally" forgotten. Busted again! With no surprise to her—just to thick-skulled me—she exposed the contraband package of chewing gum that I had disobediently placed in my lunch box.

I wallowed in guilt and fear all day long at school. Later that evening I went to my mom and asked her to forgive me. As we talked, she told me there was someone whom I had hurt even worse. That was the night I asked for forgiveness from Jesus, for my gum escapade as well as for all my sins—and I humbly received his gift of salvation.

Do you think you're free from the struggle of lying? You may be, but this temptation finds a way of creeping in, particularly when you start to feel torn between acceptance from your peers and not disappointing or getting in trouble with your parents. I can't tell you how often I've heard this kind of girl-talk:

Girl 1: "What did your parents say about *that*?"

Girl 2: "They were clueless. I told them I was doing *this*, but really we snuck out of her house and went *here* instead." (I'm sure that you can fill in the details with any number of scenarios.)

Maybe lying isn't a problem for you, but there are some other dangerous temptations linked to the mouth: dishonesty and insincerity. Even if you don't lie outright, it's easy to be dishonest or insincere. You simply sugarcoat the truth and tell people what they want to hear. Sometimes you want to avoid hurting someone's feelings, but that doesn't make dishonesty right. Being insincere is just as bad as lying because pretty soon you say things that you don't mean, which could end up doing the very thing you were trying to avoid—hurting someone.

When I was in high school, my mom often gave me a challenge before I got out of the car in the morning. I'll never forget the day she told me to compliment three people that I normally didn't talk to. *Easy*, I thought to myself: *I like your shirt*; *Your hair looks good like that*; *Nice purse*. You know, totally shallow comments. Then just as I put one foot out of the car, Mom added this: "Compliment their characters and personalities. Don't say anything you don't mean and don't lie."

In other words, she instructed me to be *genuine*. This was going to be a little more difficult than I had thought.

God's daily assignment for us is the same: to be genuine and sincere. If these deeper character traits are developed within us, then it will become very difficult to tell lies or to allow untruths to come from our mouths. It should aggravate us when we lie. We should notice it. But the more we exaggerate and talk fluff, the more desensitized we get. It is scary how easy lying can become! And God despises lying. He hates it enough to mention it twice on his list of seven hated things.

Maybe we'd be better off if lightning really did strike us when we lied or if, like Pinocchio, our noses would grow each time untruths escaped our mouths. But until this phenomenon happens, we must pray that God will help us to say only things that please him instead of things that hurt others, that are misleading or that are even bold-faced lies. Take some advice from someone who has been there: Don't be guilty of lying—especially through chocolate-covered teeth!

Anything But Plastic

. . . .

1. Which aspect of dishonesty is more tempting to you: bold-faced lying, half-truths or insincere comments? Why do you think you lie?

2. Have you ever gotten in trouble for lying or stretching the truth? Describe a situation of your own or someone else's. How does getting caught in a lie make you feel?

3. Why should lying really not be a difficult situation for Christians?

Read Leviticus 19:11. What does it say about lying?

Read Titus 1:2. What does it say about lying?

Do you think being a Christian makes the struggle with lying easier or harder? Why?

4. Have you ever had someone lie to you and you later found that person out? How did that make you feel?

What does Proverbs 12:22 say about those who are not true to their word? How do you think God views you when you are faithful to his promises?

Read Proverbs 19:9. What happens to a liar? What do you think this verse means?

Beyond Plastic . . . .

Are the words that come out of your mouth pure and honest or are you wearing chocolate crumbs? God loves sincerity and despises a lying tongue. Take the challenge of genuinely and sincerely saying nice things to three people today. Can you do it?

BEYOND THE LOOKING GLASS

Mirror.
Mind's accomplice.
A true reflection
or a distorted perception
of whomever before it stands?
Imploring eyes seek comfort there
in the looking glass.
It's not found.
Tears flow.
Mirror.

I wrote the poem above several years back at a very low point in my life. Depressed and alone, I did not like what I saw when I looked in the mirror. Did I look that much different than I do now? Probably not. But I based my dissatisfaction with myself on my perception of my reflection in the glass.

I think it was at that time that I decided mirrors are bad—the enemy. Yet I can admit that as much as I hate them, I kind of need them too! As a dancer and a dance teacher faced with a wall of mirrors, I am forced to look at my body in a leotard and tights—not my favorite thing to do! But I depend on those mirrors quite a bit to help fix flaws in body movements when dancing.

Let's take a closer look at the positives and negatives of this thing that fairy tales call the looking glass. Sometimes a mirror saves you from leaving the house with something hanging out of your nose or with the back of your skirt tucked into your underwear! On occasion it reveals a lurking pepper grain stuck in your front teeth. But consider the flip side. How many hours have you wasted standing before the mirror depressed, angry, frustrated or dissatisfied?

Mirrors force us to see blemishes on our skin, bumps in our hair and cellulite on our thighs. We pick, poke, prod, suck in, pull up, turn around, check every angle and sigh at the image we see before us. Often, when we can peel ourselves away from the glass, we go away feeling worse than we did before! Many of us begin to blame our failures, our lack of boyfriends or popularity, and our feelings of inferiority on the way we look. Is this sometimes depressing act of looking in the mirror a healthy way to spend our time?

Have you ever thought about why we can't see God? Perhaps he does not want us to judge him by the way he looks; maybe if we beheld his beauty, we would feel even more inferior to him and just quit striving to be like him; maybe we would love him less because it would decrease the mystery of the faith we have in an unseen God. Can you imagine saying, "Oh, that's just God"?

Though we can't see him, God did give us a mirror with which to judge ourselves: his heart. Is your heart a reflection of his? Do you love what he loves, hate what he hates and desire what he desires? Are you concerned about others the way he is? Do you resemble him in such a way that others see Christ in you?

Mirrors in themselves are not bad things; it's how we use them that matters. God does not put us in front of a mirror and tell us to stand there until we look exactly like him. We'd get awfully tired of standing if that were the case! What he does ask of us is to pull away from that primping mirror and park for a while in front of his image. We must spend time with him if we want to know him and love like him. Which mirror do you depend on for your encouragement and identity: God's perfect heart or that breakable, man-made looking glass?

Anything But Plastic

1. What do you spend too much time looking at in the mirror? Is there a particular part of your body that you focus on?

   Do you often spend time looking in the mirror? If so, what are some other things you could be doing with that time?

2. Let's say that you woke up tomorrow and there were no more mirrors. What would you do if mirrors were missing from your life? What type of adjustments would you have to make, for instance, when putting on makeup or going shopping for clothes? How easy would it be for you, personally, to function without mirrors?

3. You've considered how you would feel if you couldn't see yourself in a mirror. How do you feel about the fact that you can't physically see God?

Why do you think he has not shown himself to you in a physical way? What do you think your reaction would be if you could see God with your eyes?

4. Read the following verses. For each one, list the phrase that describes what aspect of God you should worship or delight in.

1 Chronicles 16:29:

Psalm 27:4:

Psalm 111:2, 3:

5. Read Genesis 1:27. Considering this verse, how should you feel about yourself?

Beyond Plastic. . . . .

It's tough when you're a girl because let's face it, girls primp! But someone will tell you about the thing stuck in your teeth. And that zit will go away. So, eyes off the flaws and onto the reflection of perfection. Looking at God will make you feel good!

MOOD RINGS

Do you know someone who is moody? Someone who causes you to walk on eggshells because you can never predict his or her reaction to the situation at hand? Perhaps you are the moody one. I know that I've been guilty of moodiness a time or two—or twenty!—before.

Everyone has a bad day every now and then. But come on, how many times have we used PMS as a great excuse for our bad moods? Eventually, people will catch on to the fact that no one has PMS every day. They will then figure out that we are moody because we are just selfish.

What? Did I just call you selfish? Yes, I did. We humans are selfish—plain and simple. We care about getting what we want, and if we don't get it, we often react badly. We are fickle; we change, we shift.

But take another look at the verse above. With Christ there is no change, no unknown side, no unpredictable behavior, no strange quirk, no shifting, no turning from who we know him to be and who his Word says that he is—never. Maybe we could just paraphrase James 1:17 to say, "Every good thing comes from God, because God is not moody!"

When our focus is directed toward ourselves, we can't even begin to see God at work around us—particularly when our moodiness sets in. You cannot supply to your own spirit and soul the encouragement, grace, faith, love, hope, compassion and joy that Christ so freely gives. Look back at James 1:17. The characteristics of the Spirit that I just mentioned are perfect illustrations of

what is good in *God's* eyes. Note also that the source of these good things is "above." The Bible does not say that you will find these good gifts inside your own moody self.

It also doesn't say that money, fame, popularity, good-looking boyfriends and new cars come from above. These may seem to be "good and perfect" gifts in our human minds, and God may choose to bless you with one or all of these good things. Or he may not. He knows what is really good and perfect for you. He is faithful to address and care for every detail of our lives. And there is another thing we can count on—our God is never moody. He is all we need, and he never changes!

Anything But Plastic

1. When is moodiness a problem for you? What causes you to be in a bad mood?

   Read Colossians 3:2. When you get moody, where does your focus tend to be? Give some examples of earthly things that you tend to focus on.

2. As you grow in your understanding of God, you will realize that your life needs to be Spirit-controlled and not emotion-driven. Read Ephesians 4:17–32. What do verses 17–19 say about ungodly people?

   What does verse 22 say you should throw off? What needs to be renewed?

   From verses 25-32, what are some of the sins mentioned there that are particularly a problem for you?

3. Wouldn't it be scary if God were as moody as people can be? Read the following Scripture verses. According to each verse, name something that God does for you or has done for his children in the Bible.

Psalm 139:16–18:

Jeremiah 29:11-13:

1 John 1:9:

4. Instead of letting yourself get in a bad mood, try thinking about all the good things God has done for you. Read Philippians 4:8. What are some things you can think about that would fall into these categories?

Beyond Plastic . . . .

Ask God to help you each day to choose thoughts and attitudes that will be positive and pleasing to him. Also ask him to nudge you the next time you use a bad mood as an excuse for your bad behavior!

GET OVER IT!

Why am I discouraged? Why so sad? I will put my hope in God!
I will praise him again—my Savior and my God!

Psalm 42:5, 6

"Get over it!"

"Suck it up!"

"Life goes on."

How many times in your life have you heard these words? Maybe when you were struggling with a friend problem, a failing grade, watching the boy you like fall for some other girl or even something more serious like your parents' divorce. As you heard this advice, did you clench your teeth in bitterness, knowing that getting on with life is so much easier said than done?

My parents had another expression they used with me all through my teenage years: "Oh no, Mieka is being a stick in the mud!" The catch is, most of the time, I deserved it. I had mastered the art of

pouting and sulking. But there is a lot of danger in this art. What often starts out as a droopy lip and sad eyes soon affects your heart and turns into a bad case of moping. So whenever I fell into moping, my dad in particular had a way of drawing those words out so that (a) I knew he didn't feel sorry for me and (b) I started to feel embarrassed of my attitude.

You could say that Samuel faced the same problem of moping. It was easy to see how he fell prey to this problem. Samuel had been such a faithful servant of God. He had worked with Saul, mentoring him, spending time with him and guiding him. He had even anointed Saul to be king. But after all of Samuel's faithfulness and dedication, Saul disobeyed and God chose to reject Saul from kingship. Just think about all that Sam had put into this project, only to have it crash down on him. First Samuel 15:35 tells us that Samuel mourned constantly after this. He became a mope. But God looked at his servant Samuel and said, "Get over it!" (See 1 Samuel 16:1.)

God desires his servants to be in tune with him. Just like Samuel, when we mope, our hearts sink, we lose our focus and become less useful in God's service. Sticks in the mud are just not that effective as servants for Christ! From studying this Scripture passage, I realized that God calls us to be prepared to serve him in two ways: in mind and in action.

God had to say to Samuel, "Look! Stop mourning!" When we are down in the dumps and all absorbed in ourselves, our minds and hearts cannot listen for God's call. Secondly, God told Samuel to be prepared physically, to get his things together so he could do what God needed him to do. God has given you certain talents, abilities and gifts that he wants you to use. It's hard to keep these in good condition when you are moping. He wants you to be physically on the ball so he can put you into action at any time!

When I endured a major disappointment in my career, I definitely mourned. And what else did I do? I moped. I stuck out my lip and wallowed in my misery. But then God shook me and said, "Hey, Mieka! You're being a stick in the mud! How long will you pout? Get up. Stop feeling sorry for yourself and be ready for the *other* things that I have prepared for you to do."

So I did what God wanted! I shook it off, stuck my lip back in and put my eyes back on him. And I've been amazed ever since. It was shortly thereafter that God called me to begin working on this book. I am so excited to see what God will do with the rest of my life. And you can have the same feeling. Just trust that God has the best plans for you. Remember, if you're stuck in the mud, you won't get very far!

Anything But Plastic

1. There is a definite difference between moping and mourning. I think you'll always go through instances of both of these in your life. What are some times in your life when you have moped?

   What about mourning? Are there some unfortunate circumstances in your past that caused genuine grief and mourning—perhaps the loss of a loved one, a divorce, etc.? Name several instances in your life where you took some time to mourn.

2. Read Nehemiah 8:9-12. Why were the people told not to weep? What is going to be their strength?

3. In each of the following verses, what replaces sorrow and mourning? Who makes this happen?

   Esther 9:22:

   Psalm 30:11:

Jeremiah 31:10-14:

4. Read Isaiah 60:20. What happens to your mourning when the everlasting light is in your life? Think of a time when God replaced your mourning with joy. How did this happen? What helped you to get over your grief?

5. How can you help others move on from grief and know God's joy?

Beyond Plastic . . . .

Don't throw pity parties. It's OK and even good to mourn at times, but don't let disappointment take over your life and turn you into a mope. Put your hope in God. He can take you from being a downright downer to a dancing fool!

MYSTERY MAN

I love this verse. It is so full of mystery. It's as if God is reminding me, *Mieka, I don't want you to know everything that is going on, or the whys and wherefores of your life. I want you to look at me and what I am doing and say, "I can't figure it out!"*

God is mysterious. He uses that elusiveness to draw me closer to him. He calls me to trust him even though it is an intangible faith that binds me to him. I cannot touch God. I cannot physically see him with my eyes. I cannot see what he is doing. But because I have faith in him and his Word gives me promise after promise of his presence, I trust that God is there. As Jesus reminds me in his Word, I cannot see the wind, but I know it is there because of the effects it has on the things around it (John 4:8). Trees sway with the wind's rhythm, leaves scatter from contact with the wind, and goose bumps pop up when the wind hits your skin. These are all visible results of the work of an invisible force.

God's intangible and invisible being is like the wind. We can't see it with our eyes, but its effects on our lives are felt everywhere. I cannot see his love for me, but he sent his Son to die for me, so I know that is love. I cannot always see the plans that he has for me, but he put me here on this earth, so I can take that as proof that he has work for me to do. I did not see God create the majesty of this world. But when the trees change color, it reflects the beauty of his creation. The seasons dance in and out, their splendor giving honor to God—yet again providing proof that

God designed our world. So, although we cannot see the intangible, the longer we bask in God's presence, the more we should be able to sense and proclaim that God is close.

We all have hopes and dreams for our future. Sometimes it's hard not knowing what's going to happen, or when. But God does not intend for us to know ahead of time exactly the choices and timing of the things he has ordained for us. What kind of faith would we have if we knew all the details of God's agenda? Would our relationships with him be as deep and as meaningful if we didn't have to depend on him?

What we can know is that God knows our heart's desires. And what we can do is pray about those and trust that God will give us just what we need, at just the right time. One of my heart's desires is to meet God's choice of a mate for me. And even though I don't know where my future husband is, I still pray for him, and I don't doubt that God is preparing what's best for me.

Of course, I still ask questions. Have I done something wrong? Has God got work left for me to do on my own? The *answers* to these questions may never come, but the book of Ecclesiastes encourages me that *God's timing* will come! There is a time and a purpose for everything!

Until things become clearer, I lean on Ecclesiastes 3:11. What are you waiting for? You can wonder about when it might happen, but don't worry about it. God's timing is perfect. Wouldn't you rather be subject to his perfect timing than to your own imperfect plans?

Anything But Plastic

1. What do you desire in your life? Is there a goal you are shooting for? a certain grade? a certain position in a school sport or club? the healing of a sick family member?

2. What is your attitude toward God as you wait for his answers to these things? Do you let Satan get you down at times? Is your faith ever shaken as a result of God's silence?

3. Read 1 Timothy 3:9. What type of truths does Paul describe regarding faith?

   Read Hebrews 11:1–3. What definition is given of faith? What does this mean to you?

4. Write a thought regarding each of the following. If you cannot *touch* these things, then how do you know they are real?

How do you know that someone loves you?

How do you know that a sick person has hope?

How do you know that a Christian has faith?

5. In closing, read 1 Peter 1:8. Even though you cannot see Christ, what should you do?

What should your attitude be as you believe and hope in your intangible God?

Beyond Plastic . . . .

While you're waiting for some answers, try reading God's Word and talking to him. Remember, all things are made perfect in his time!

MEET THE PARENTS

You children must always obey your parents,
for this is what pleases the Lord.

Colossians 3:20

"Shut up!"

"Leave me alone!"

"That's so unfair!"

"I hate you!"

Words like these usually slip quickly off of the tongue, land with a sting on the ears of the listeners and linger in the air, often followed by bedroom doors slamming. Are you guilty of yelling these or similar things at your parents? Maybe you do the opposite—ignoring your mom and dad, refusing to answer their questions or to give them the time of day.

As teenagers, you are faced with the persistent presence of parents in your lives. They ask you questions, they poke for information, they tell you what to do and what not to do. This can be overwhelming and annoying. You are in a stage of life where most people desire to have their own identity and independence. Maybe your response to the parental presence is to keep yourself locked up in your bedroom. Maybe you rebel and experiment with everything your parents tell you not to do—you sneak out, you come home past curfew. Perhaps you disobey even the smallest of requests, such as getting off the telephone or computer.

Do you know that teenagers in the Bible faced similar struggles to yours? Read Luke 15 and take a look at the prodigal son. This kid took money from his father, left the safety net of his home and went off unsupervised. That would be the life, right? He thought he could enjoy himself more and would be better off on his own, without the presence of his parents. But as Jesus tells, he began living loosely. He played too hard, selfishly spent all of his money and became so desperate that he realized the only person who could help him was the very one he had run from. In humility, he came back to apologize and make himself his father's slave.

When you disobey your parents, how often do you have a genuine change of heart and apologize to them? How often do you say, "I have done wrong. I hurt you. I am no longer worthy to be your daughter. I don't deserve your love; I don't deserve anything you can give me; you should treat me like a hired worker." Not hardly! The typical reaction is to let your disobedience and unkind words just slide by until the next time you get angry.

Now look at the response of the father in this story. The obnoxious behavior of the son did not cause Dad to slam doors, drive off screeching down the road or threaten never to buy his son anything ever again. Why? Because he loved his son so much that before the son could even apologize, the father was throwing a party to welcome him home. Dad ran to his boy, embraced him, kissed him, dressed him to the nines, brought out the best food, cranked up the music and danced.

How often do your parents treat you as if you never did wrong or hurt their feelings? They continue to provide for you, sometimes neglecting their own needs. God knew what he was doing when he gave us parents. They've been in our shoes; they were once teenagers and had parents of their own. God gave them the responsibility of loving and caring for us, and with that comes the job of disciplining us. Let's face it, all discipline pretty much stinks at the time, but it teaches us and makes us who we are.

The prodigal son realized that he was wrong and still had much to learn from his earthly parents. He needed them. When was the last time you crawled up and sat on your dad's lap? When was the last time you let your mom tuck you in or stroke your hair? It is OK to need help; it is OK to want to feel loved. No matter how old I get, there will never be anything like crawling up into my daddy's lap and crying on his shoulder.

As long as our parents are alive, we are still their children and we are still accountable to them. Don't run from your parents' discipline like the prodigal son did. He learned his lesson the hard way. Parents are a gift from God. You can be thankful for your gift every day through your joyful obedience to God and to his earthly authority over you.

. . . .

1. Read the story of the prodigal son in Luke 15:11–32. What did it take to break the son's pride? Do you really think the son was repentant? Why or why not?

2. Read Ephesians 6:1–3. What expectations or rules do your parents have for you that aggravate you? When do you find it most difficult to obey them?

List three reasons why you think your parents have guidelines for you.

3. For some of us, it's our human nature to be curious about and rebel against rules. Read Romans 1:28–32. What does verse 28 say God did as a result of the peoples' sin? List some of the sins and temptations the people fell into. What does verse 32 say is the penalty for these sins?

Whoa! Disobedience to parents is ranked up there with wickedness, greed, evil and murder!? So how do you think God feels when you mistreat Mom and Dad?

4. Is there a time you *reluctantly* obeyed your parents but were later very thankful for their direction and protection over you? Describe the situation.

Beyond Plastic . . . .

Jesus was obedient to his Father. He loved his Father so much that he died on the cross for you. Remembering Jesus' example of obedience to his Father, what can you do in your generation to show your parents that you really do love them, despite how you act towards them at times? Ask God to help you desire to be willingly obedient to your parents and to respond to them with love and respect. He can make it happen!

PARTY GIRLS

You are to live clean, innocent lives as children of God in a dark world full of crooked and perverse people. Let your lives shine brightly before them.

Philippians 2:15

To party or not to party? That is the question. I'm not talking about birthday parties with cake and ice cream. I'm talking about the ones with alcohol, drugs, kids trashing someone's house and people having sex upstairs. Maybe parties aren't a problem for you as a Christian at all. But I'll bet they are. One of the hardest things I ever dealt with as a teenager was this party dilemma.

I am one of those people who actually loved high school. I had a blast meeting new people. I loved making someone laugh or noticing when people were having a bad day and trying to encourage them. I just liked people, no matter who they were!

My parents raised me to believe that as a Christian I needed to love people, but not necessarily love what they *did*. You know the old saying—love the sinner, but not the sin. So for that reason, I made friends with all kinds of people regardless of what walk of life they were from, the filthy mouths they had or their social activities. But many of these school friendships were choked by a boundary— the school walls.

When that school bell rang on Friday and the weekend began, I no longer shared most of the same activities with the people who just five seconds ago I called my friends. There was always this social issue of *the party* that loomed over my head like a little black cloud. I can't count the number of times I attempted to convince people that dinner and a movie on a Friday night could actually be fun.

Or how many times I was dying to go out with those weekday friends.

At times I thought I could maybe go to the parties and just blend but not participate in the festivities. This was doable right? After all, everyone knew my convictions and how I felt about things. People knew how important being a Christian was to me.

So if my classmates just saw me at a party, they would automatically know I only came there to hang out. They would know without a doubt that I wasn't chugging a beer, smoking a ciggy or doing drugs. Right? My reputation could surely remain unharmed. Right?

The problem is that people that are in the process of "getting sloshed" and "having a good time," whatever that entails, are not going to stop and notice that you are an upstanding good Christian who is *not* doing anything bad. They will just notice that you are there. The majority of partygoers aren't sober enough to give the nonparticipants some credit. In their minds—you're there, having a good time too! Have you ever heard the expression "guilty by association"?

Believe me, I *wanted* to go! I wanted to be with my friends, laughing and having fun. I wanted to be a part of all of the jokes on Monday that were only funny to the people who were there on Friday.

But after much prayer and many tears, I knew I had to choose. I really wasn't ever tempted to drink or smoke or do any of those things. That just wasn't the problem for me. But I did have to decide whether or not being a friend of the "in" crowd was more important to me than my reflection of Christ to others. So I chose not to go.

Was this decision easy? No! On top of being considered a goody-goody or a nerd, I hated other things about it. I missed out on being a part of the inside jokes. People wouldn't tell me stuff because they were afraid I'd judge them. My decision to stick to my convictions haunted me. I felt an inch tall when people said things like, "Oh, don't bother asking Mieka. She won't go."

Then again, high school is a crazy place to be. You know—you're familiar with the territory. Now, from this vantage point, no matter how many tears I cried and how much pain I thought I was in, I'm still proud of my decision to back away from certain things. I look back now and see in hindsight that people did respect me for those decisions—that even though those kids made fun of me, they just didn't understand, and they sometimes even admired me from afar. (People will tell you all kinds of things at high school reunions!)

I understand the frustration that confronts you in making decisions like these. I know all about the burning desire you have just to be liked, to feel accepted, to go to the parties and the places where people hang out—just to feel like you are kind of on the outside edge of the inside crowd. But I encourage you to stick with the Bible's instruction to be *in* the world, but not *of* it. People will take notice of you. If they don't understand you, so be it. Maybe you'll have a chance to show them that Christ is your reason for doing what you do. Isn't that one of God's purposes for leaving us here on this earth—to point others to him, regardless of how strange they may think we are? It's OK to be different—in the world, but not just like the world. Remember—original, not plastic!

Anything But Plastic

1. Is this party thing an issue that you have been confronted with yet? What do you think the expression "Be in the world, but not of the world" means? Give some examples that you think define this statement.

2. How do you stand out from others around you? What makes you different in a good way?

   Are there areas where you might blend in with the world a little more than you should? What are these?

3. Many Christians argue that they can go to a party and not participate in any of the activities. They say they could go with the purpose of standing out and being different. Although this may work on a *rare* occasion, can you think of some reasons why it might not work at all?

4. Read John 14:31. How will the world know you love God?

Read John 18:36. What does this verse say about God's kingdom?

Read 1 John 3:1, which tells us that the world will not know or understand us. Why not?

5. What can you do to help others understand the things you do for Christ?

Beyond Plastic

Life is full of decisions and being a teenager is hard. But basically you have two choices: live by the world's standards, or by God's. Which do you choose?

GET OUT THE AIRBRUSH

Each time he said, "My gracious favor is all you need. My power works best in your weakness." So now I am glad to boast about my weaknesses, so that the power of Christ may work through me.

2 Corinthians 12:9

Look around you, grab your magazines, check out the billboards as you're driving down the freeway, and flip on the TV for an endless supply of makeover shows and the latest Hollywood update. What do you see? Flawless girls with large breasts, low-ride waistlines, bony hips, skinny waists, tan bodies, luscious lips, perfectly colored hair and not a zit in sight! And what's the incentive for obtaining this perfection? Why, the shirtless guys with the perfectly tousled hair, ripped abs, intense eyes and killer smiles, of course! That's the reward when you obtain perfection, right? And if it works for them, maybe it will work for you. *Right?!*

What extremes will we go to as we stare at these figures and think, *I want to look just like her*? Perhaps Botox, liposuction, collagen injections, breast enhancement, tans in a bottle, tans from a booth, magic weight loss pills, laxatives, low-carb diets, don't-eat-anything diets, trips to the dermatologist and trips to the gym. After all of this effort to achieve perfection, does the knight in shining armor show up? Or is it just the disappointment and depression that sets in when we realize that our imperfections are still glaringly obvious?

I really have no clue where I got the idea that I have to be perfect at *everything* I do. It isn't that I think Christ expects perfection from me—I know better than that! Deep down in my heart, I know that perfection does not exist outside of Christ. Only Christ can be so holy and entirely unblemished. Nevertheless, I often find myself striving for my absolute best in almost every aspect of my life: my looks, my job, my relationships with people and even in my relationship with God. Sadly enough, I always feel like a loser when I fail to live up to my own unrealistic expectations.

What freaks me out as much as expecting perfection from myself is the thought that others sometimes expect me to be perfect as well. A student of mine once insisted that I was perfect—no matter how much I tried to dispel her totally inaccurate view!

If I were perfect, I could roll out of bed and head out in the morning without a bit of attention to personal hygiene. I would never feel insecure, wondering if the reason I can't find that perfect guy is because I'm not skinny or pretty enough. My clothing size wouldn't annoy me, and I would look like a model in every outfit I tried on.

If I were perfect, I would do everything right the first time I tried it. I wouldn't have to go to ballet class in order to improve my skills. I wouldn't have to watch what I say—I'd never hurt the feelings of my family and friends, and, therefore, would never need to apologize for thoughtless or hurtful words.

But—if I were perfect, I would never encourage myself with Scripture and memorize it in order to keep Satan from defeating me. I would never meet different kinds of people and gain all sorts of experiences if I already had the perfect job, the perfect church ministry and the perfect boyfriend. And I wouldn't need to spend time with God, because he wouldn't have any more lessons to teach me.

Are you beginning to get the picture? Without any of my human flaws, life would be effortless—absolutely *no problema*! But then again, if I were physically perfect, I would be boring, unoriginal—a mere replica of the glitzy images of perfection that we see all around. I wouldn't be *me*. And it seems to me that perfectly beautiful people don't often look for their confidence in Christ. Perfectly acting people wouldn't sin—and people without sin don't need Christ's love and forgiveness. Our imperfections are God's means of keeping us focused on the only one who *is* perfect.

So then we read this verse, Matthew 5:48: "You are to be perfect, even as your Father in heaven is perfect." Wait a minute—isn't that a contradiction to what we've just been discussing?

At first glance this command may seem impossible to follow. But the Bible doesn't define perfection the way magazines do. God doesn't ask us to have tan bodies, smooth skin and lush lips to attract the perfect guy. He requires that we be perfectly *mature* and *complete* in his likeness with a *goal* of living a sinless life, not that we be physically flawless. What a relief to know that being perfect in Christ doesn't require liposuction, tummy tucks or plastic surgery!

What's more, God doesn't expect flawed creatures like us to just start acting perfectly on our own. We have his example to guide us, his words to instruct us and his love to motivate us. God says that we are works in progress that he is not finished with yet—thank goodness! God's desires for us are attainable and valuable—unlike the world's!

I recently discovered that the average actress takes two-and-a-half hours to get ready to walk down the red carpet. Only after several hair and makeup artists go to work on her is she ready for the cameras. Even in trying to get my picture taken for this book, I was shocked when the photographer said she could use her computer to airbrush away stray strands of hair, cover up a zit, make my hips narrower and my eyes brighter—and I'm not even a model! Just imagine what our "ideal" beauties must go through before their pictures appear on those glossy magazine covers.

The images of perfection that this world is plastered with are nothing more than plastic imitations of the real thing. God does not expect you to be without flaws but simply to be the total and whole person that he created you to be. Being a whole person sounds way less stressful than having to be a perfect person, don't you think? Accept your flaws and trash the airbrush. Then you will truly be an original girl in this plastic world!

Anything But Plastic

1. Mr. Webster defines the word *perfect* as follows.

   perfect: complete in all respects; without defect; flawless; in a condition of complete excellence

   Just imagine these perfect things:
   The perfect day . . .
   The perfect outfit . . .
   The perfectly decorated room . . .
   The perfect vacation . . .
   The perfect date . . .
   The perfect car . . .
   The perfect boyfriend . . .
   But a truly perfect person?

2. Name one or two people you admire now or admired when you were younger and considered to be perfect or close-to-perfect people. What do you see in these people that makes them *seem* perfect to you? Be specific.

3. You know that these people aren't really perfect. Nobody is. What types of things do humans do that reveal our imperfections to others?

And what about you? What weaknesses or struggles do you have that you camouflage in order to appear perfect? Do you hide a fear of some kind? a habit?

4. Since we don't seem to measure up, let's take a look at someone who is perfect—God! Read Deuteronomy 32:4. What does it say about the Rock?

5. Read 2 Corinthians 12:9, 10. When does it say that God gives power to his children? What should we boast about? What happens when we are weak?

Read Matthew 5:48. What does this verse say that you are to be? We already discussed that this is not possible according to the world's standards. What do you think this verse is really asking of you in particular?

Beyond Plastic . . . .

Take a few minutes to talk to God. Focus on your idea of perfection and how it fits into your life. Surrender to God the areas that you want him to mature and make more complete in him.

PLAYING FORT

This I declare of the Lord: He alone is my refuge, my place of safety; he is my God, and I am trusting in him.

Psalm 91:2

Do you ever wish you lived in the days of knights and castles? Bulwarks and fortresses are foreign to most of us unless we travel to Europe and explore ancient palaces or see these in movies. We will never sense the danger of the bad guy pursuing us over the castle walls. We will never experience the rush of hiding behind protective ramparts. Moats and iron gates are things of the past. But I know someone who is still in the business of building castles.

In Psalm 91 God reminds us of his total protection over us. Even in this day and age, with our modern alarm systems, advanced weapons and well-trained police forces, we are still encouraged to dwell in Christ and in his mighty fortress as he stands guard over us.

Several years ago, a group of friends (ranging in age from the mid-twenties to mid-thirties) and I decided to build a fort. We're talking about a major, all-out, fort-building fest. We came prepared with supplies of staplers, tape and bedsheets; we even had T-shirts made that said "Fort Night '99" on them. We architects took our fort-building job seriously, stapling and rearranging until we transformed an entire living room into the fort that would serve as our Friday night escape. We anchored our construction strongly, stocked the inside and secured our entrance. After all, this fort would serve as our refuge for the next five hours.

Inside our protective quarters we took blankets, pillows, food and drinks. We hoarded the TV, movies, gum, tissues and anything else we could think of. Then for a brief time, we laughed, relaxed and rested, completely forgetting about the outside world. We resided in our fortress and feared no attack from beyond those walls. We had confidence that what we had built would not fall and that as long as we remained within the hanging sheets, safety prevailed.

If I can place my safety for an evening in a fort made of bed linens, how much more should I rejoice in the protection that my God offers me? I am overwhelmed by God's "bigness," particularly when I read through Psalm 91. This passage overflows with promises of protection. God offers to be our shelter, shadow, refuge, fortress, pinion, shield, bulwark and dwelling place. We are talking about some heavy-duty coverage over our lives!

Yet sometimes we forget about our castle-building friend, and when life gets hard and difficult circumstances surround us, we run every which way in search of a place to retreat. Perhaps you go to your bedroom or get into your car and drive anywhere in search of shelter.

In the meantime, God's fort is open twenty-four hours a day and is always ready for visitors. He is waiting for us to rest and dwell in him as he stands guard at the door, prepared to keep anyone from disturbing the peace he so readily offers his children. All we need is truly to choose to dwell there. Take up refuge in God, for unlike my friends and my fort made of sheets, his fort is indestructible and a strong place where you can rest. Won't you escape there?

Anything But Plastic

1. Read Psalm 91 once or twice through. You might even try reading it out loud. How do the words used to describe God make you feel about the fact that he is your protector? Which aspects of God's character strike you the most?

2. What current circumstances have made you concerned, worried or stressed? How do you think that God wants to demonstrate these Psalm 91 qualities to you even now?

   What do you think happens to your heart that might keep God's love and power from getting through?

3. When you were growing up, did you ever build a fort? What did you like about playing fort?

4. What are some types of fortresses that people tend to substitute for God's protection? What type of false fortresses do you build in your life?

5. How does it feel to know that God wants to protect you?

Beyond Plastic . . . .

Pick out some of the verses from Psalm 91 that mean a lot to you and memorize them. Remember, God is always watching over you—let go and allow him to be your great refuge.

ANYTIME MINUTES

Keep on praying.

You sail through the subdivision going 20 miles over the speed limit, and as the cop magically appears from behind the trees, you desperately cry out, "Oh, Lord, please don't let me get a ticket; please don't let me get a ticket!!!"

Or how about this one. You arrive at school on Monday morning, and a girl from your math class asks if you studied for your test. When you remember the weekend you spent hanging with your friends instead of studying, you pray, "O Heavenly Father, please help me pass my math test! I can't afford to fail it!"—even though you know you didn't study a bit.

Or you're leaving the party on Friday night. As you hop into the car to head home, you realize you smell like a walking cigarette or the beer that someone spilled on you. (Maybe it was *your* cigarette or beer.) As the smell fills the car, you pray, "O Lord, please don't let me get caught; please let my parents be in bed."

All of the above examples exhibit the art of "SOS praying." As stubborn, independent humans, we so often only turn to prayer out of last-minute desperation. Perhaps we pray only when we need something. Maybe our pleas are strictly Sunday-sent when we go to church. That's not to say that God doesn't want us to cry out to him when we do need something or when we are desperate. But he also expects and longs for another level of deeper and more intimate prayer.

In 1 Thessalonians, Paul tells us to keep on praying, without stopping. That

Anytime Minutes

sounds like an awfully long time to spend in prayer. In some Bible footnotes this ceaseless prayer is even compared to a hacking cough. I can relate! Since I was young, I have always been able to detect an oncoming cold or a sinus infection. My family has become experts at predicting my illness as well. We all know, because I get this annoying little hacking cough. It's not very loud or obnoxious. It's really more like a sputter—it's hardly worth the effort. But once my throat starts to tickle, I'm stuck with this nagging cough for the duration of my sickness. I can forget inhaling through my mouth, because once the air hits my throat, I hack away even more.

So what does coughing have to do with prayer? Paul's words remind us of the importance of the *habit* of prayer. This means not just throwing up desperate SOS prayers whenever we get stuck in bad situations. We need to have an attitude and frame of mind that recognize God's availability to listen to us, and our need to pray, at all times. Setting aside a period of time daily to talk with him is also a great idea, but we don't have to save prayer only for scheduled moments. We can pray in church, at home, in the car, through laughter, through tears and trials, in our times of loneliness and times of joy, during stressful circumstances, in

sickness, in health and yes, in panic! If it comes to mind, voice it to him. If you see a beautiful sunset, thank him. If someone hurts you, cry on God's shoulder. You don't even have to wait for the nighttime or weekend rates to kick in. Pray anytime. Just keep on praying!

So often, though, once we get out of the habit of prayer, we feel guilty. We may believe it is too late to recover our open communication with God. Because of this, our prayer life becomes almost nonexistent. But it is never too late. God never cuts us off. He's always ready for us to talk to him, even if it's just to say, "Sorry, God. I'll try to do better." When times are hard or confusing, God still desires you to come to him. Whether you can feel it or not, God is working on your behalf from the moment you utter the prayer.

I long to be a fervent prayer warrior, knowing that I have constant access to God, 24/7. Psalm 55:17 says, "Morning, noon, and night I plead aloud in my distress, and the Lord hears my voice." I don't know why I sometimes have such a hard time disciplining myself to have a solid prayer time, but I'd be doing better if I prayed as much as I cough and sputter! Prayer is not just for bedtimes, mealtimes and last-minute emergencies. Do you want to give this "hacking cough" a try?

Anything But Plastic

1. If you had to describe your prayer life in a phrase or two, how would you do it? Are you pleased with the discipline of your prayer life? Why or why not?

2. There are so many examples of people in the Bible who had passionate and active prayer lives. What do you think modern-day conveniences such as money, doctors, cars, etc. have done to our dependence on God?

   Read Philippians 4:6, 7. Have you ever felt peace after praying? Describe that time.

3. What drives you to pray? In other words, when are you more likely to pray? Do you think you are more of an SOS pray-er or a hacking prayer warrior? Explain.

   Prayer has many functions. Look up the following verses and make a note as to what can be done in prayer.

   Psalm 5:1-3, 8:

   Psalm 66:16-20:

   Psalm 119:169-172:

   Philippians 4:6:

4. Sometimes praying is difficult. It is easy to get distracted and let your mind wander. What struggles and frustrations do you have regarding prayer?

What do you think you should do when it seems that God isn't answering your prayers?

To stay focused when you pray, sometimes it is helpful to talk out loud, write down your requests or to envision God sitting before you. What can you do to make your prayer time more active and consistent?

5. The last aspect of prayer we need to look at is that of praying for each other. Once you take your eyes off of yourself, you are often able to see God moving in ways that you couldn't have before.

Read Romans 12:9-15. What can you do for others by praying for them?

Read Philippians 1:3-6. What does Paul do for those he mentions?

Why do you think it is important to pray for others?

Beyond Plastic . . . .

Prayer is a responsibility and a privilege. Stop and spend a moment in prayer right now. Ask God to teach you how to be more of a consistent, hacking, anytime pray-er, rather than an SOS pray-er. Ask him to help make your prayer time something that you long for on a daily basis. God is waiting just for you!

DADDY'S LITTLE PRINCESS

Praise the Lord, I tell myself, and never forget the good things he does for me. He forgives all my sins. . . . and surrounds me with love and tender mercies. He fills my life with good things.

Psalm 103:2-5

You know those days when you just feel worthless—good for nothing? The kind of day when no matter how hard you work at it, it's still a "bad hair day"? After picking out the perfect outfit, you start your period unexpectedly and have to smoothly get out of that situation. The kind of day where no matter how hard you try, you just can't say the right thing. The kind where you feel dog-ugly compared to the girl next to you who is getting attention from the guy who you think should *really* be looking at you.

Do you have those days where you want to cry out, "Just let me go back to bed! Nobody would notice if I just disappeared for a day"? In all of this mess, even if you feel anything *but* valuable, the fact remains—God sees you as a princess.

That's right—a princess! How your hair looks doesn't bother him; he isn't upset that you ruined your best outfit. God sees you and treats you as royalty. In some Bible translations, Psalm 103 says that he *crowns* you with lovingkindness and righteousness.

Is it just me, or is it difficult to picture the King of kings placing a crown on the heads of lowly humans like you and me? Compare it, let's say, to a coronation for earthly royalty, like the Queen of England. When this momentous event occurs, look out! We're talking about a big deal! The decorations go up, the red carpet rolls out, security tightens around the event, family and spectators dress in their best attire, the tiaras are polished, people come from all over to watch and the subjects bow in humble submission to the honoree.

With this in mind, how does the thought of receiving a crown from the God of *all creation* make you feel? It makes me a bit nervous. I certainly don't feel worthy. Who am I? I'm not rich. I don't come from a long line of earthly noblemen. I'm not an aristocrat. People don't step aside when I enter the room unless I've forgotten my deodorant that morning. People don't jump up and give me the best seat in a theatre or a plane just because I've decided to grace them with my presence.

So what's the deal? Scripture doesn't ever name us as princesses, does it? Well, no. But it makes it clear that we belong to God and he has chosen us. Christ in his compassion loves us enough to claim us as his own, to see us as special, as royalty, and as worthy of a crown from him, the King above all kings!

So the next time that you feel less than wonderful, grab your tiara of lovingkindness and the jewels of righteousness and let them sparkle as you strut your stuff. God wants you to be confident as his princess. He desires that you allow his blessings to flow on you and through you. So no matter what kind of "bad hair day" you're having, you'll always be Christ's royal beauty!

Anything But Plastic

1. I love the movie *Roman Holiday*. It's the one where Audrey Hepburn plays a princess who really desires just to be normal. Would you like to be an earthly princess? Why or why not?

2. Read Ephesians 1:4-6. How does it make you feel to know that the king of the universe has always wanted you in his family?

   Now read verses 7-18. What inheritance do we have in Christ, and how was it purchased for us?

3. On any ordinary day, do you feel like a princess? What stops you from feeling like royalty?

Do you ever think that God wouldn't want you? Sometimes when we sin, we may feel this way. But read Romans 5:6-11. When does verse 8 say God sent Christ to die for us?

How does this make you feel?

4. What good things has God filled your life with lately? What has God given you that *should* make you feel like a princess, even when you don't?

5. Do you act like a princess? (In a good way!) How might your behavior toward other people need to change, knowing that you are God's princess and an ambassador of his kingdom?

Beyond Plastic

In this beauty contest, you don't have to be jealous of a winner! There's room in God's court for all of his princesses. Aren't you grateful that you were born into such royalty? What inner gift or attribute can you shine on others to let them know that you have been crowned a child of God? Share God's loving mercy with someone today.

NOWHERE TO RUN

I imagine if Jonah was still alive today he could tell some stories! I mean, what is it like to put a boatful of men at the brink of death? What would he say about the waters that engulfed him and forced him to the depths of the ocean? What do things look like from the inside of a giant fish? Was it scary? dark? cold? smelly? Were there creepy, crawly things inside?

But I'd really like to ask him, "What were you thinkin'?" Did he think it was really possible to hide from God? However, Jonah just did what many believers do all the time—he ran. God asked him to do something, and Jonah responded to God's call by running in the opposite direction.

I can think of several reasons why we might try to escape the job God calls us to do. Sometimes it's a fear of failure.

Maybe we don't tell others about Christ because we're afraid we'll mess up the message, be mocked by people and, in the end, disappoint God.

Sometimes we are just plain too scared to face the unknown. Maybe we don't want to go on a mission trip because we have no clue what to expect. What if God calls us to go to a foreign land and a foreign people? What kind of trouble will we encounter on the way? Will we even make it through the journey alive? Thoughts such as these often hold us back from many great adventures.

Or perhaps we just don't like the task at hand. Maybe God gives us an assignment, and we just find the idea unpleasant. Sometimes we are happy to serve God—as long as we get to pick the service project.

It seems that this last reason was Jonah's problem. Nineveh was the capital city of the most powerful empire at that time, and the Ninevites were a pretty rough crowd. It's pretty obvious from chapter 4 of his book that Jonah didn't care for the people. He even got angry with God for saving them!

So when God first asked him to go to them, Jonah ran. No matter what his reason, the truth is that it was disobedience, plain and simple. When we disobey God's call, even if we just say, "Not right now, God!" there are always consequences. We probably won't get swallowed up by a giant fish, but we may miss out on some great experiences God had lined up for us. Or we may hurt others, without even knowing it. Just think what would have happened to the Ninevites if Jonah hadn't taken God's message to them—total destruction!

And let's suppose that that giant fish, which was instrumental in God's attempt to get through Jonah's thick skull, had disobeyed. Wait a minute—a disobedient whale? That sounds fishy! Read your Bible again. The animal was not out for a casual swim and just happened to find a man in the water. God arranged for that fish to swallow Jonah. In response to God's assignment, the beast could have said, "God, I'd rather just swim," or "No thanks, I don't want any company," or "I'm not hungry for runaway man today."

But the fish obeyed without delay, immediately swallowing Jonah up. Fortunately for him, and the city of Nineveh, God gave Jonah a second chance. Jonah was very blessed that God saw him as a valuable enough instrument to call on him a second time. Jonah received a do-over!

I am afraid that I am not always that lucky. Sometimes my God gives me two or three chances to obey, to put my trust in him or to step back and allow him to work his plan. What a wonderful God I have that he would be that patient with me! But I know in my heart that he would prefer that I got it right the first time. When I put off a task God calls me to do, or try to run away, all I am really doing in the big scheme of things is disobeying. People say that hindsight is 20/20. Could he have foreseen his rough night on the sea, being eaten alive, and having a near brush with death, I'll bet Jonah would have reconsidered his first response to God's call. His list of traumatic events is enough to make me jump to and get busy!

What about you? Is there something God is calling you to do? Are you running from him? procrastinating? Don't be disobedient. Do it now!

Anything But Plastic

1. How would you, in your own words, define the following: *obedience* and *disobedience?*

2. I mentioned three reasons for disobedience. Why do you think that you disobey? Remember, disobedience does not have to be outright rebellion. It could be something as simple as a timing issue or an attitude. Do you think that the reasons you disobey your parents are different from the reasons you disobey God?

   What effect do you think your own disobedience has on your personal life, your relationship with God and the achievement of your goals?

3. Read the following verses. For each one, write down what happened as a result of disobedience for the people in these Scriptures.

   1 Samuel 15:23:

Jeremiah 44:22, 23:

Daniel 9:10-14:

4. Read the following verses and describe what happens as a result of obedience.

Isaiah 1:19:

Job 36:11:

Jeremiah 42:6:

5. Sometimes God may only give you that one shot. Unlike Jonah, he may not call you again to do the same task, and you could miss out on being used and incredibly blessed by him. What do you need to obey God about today?

Beyond Plastic . . . .

Obeying the Lord doesn't make you a prisoner chained to a boring life! Obedience brings blessing, blessing, blessing!!! So if you've been putting off one of God's tasks for you, make it right with him today. Don't delay! You may be missing out.

THIRSTY?

Do not stifle the Holy Spirit.

1 Thessalonians 5:19

OK, all of you TV watchers and you hip magazine-readers. Here is a test for you to see how well you know your stuff; to see if the advertisers have done their jobs—to jingle their way into the databank of your memory. I'm going to list a series of commercial slogans and your job is to identify as many products as possible from the mottos that I mention:

1. It's an Up thing!
2. Obey your thirst.
3. Hungry for life, thirsty for _____.
4. Put it in your head.
5. It's just what the Doctor ordered.
6. Just for the taste of it . . .
7. Do the Dew!
8. Does your body good.
9. Generation Next
10. The joy of cola
11. Is it in you?

How well did you do? If you are a young person who is even just wading, let alone swimming, in pop culture, you probably raked in the points with your guesses—all of the way from 7-Up® to Dr. Pepper® and on down through Gatorade®. Why did you score so well? I have two guesses. First, you're a teenager. Teens are hip and current with all of the latest trends and expressions. I think God must have wired you that way. Second, advertisers appeal to your senses by using things that stick.

Almost every one of the products I mentioned is attempting to sell a method for quenching or "stifling" your thirst. After all, it's not good for your body to be depleted of the fluids it needs in order to function properly. It's miserable being thirsty. Your mouth gets dry, you can't swallow well, it's hard to focus, you feel like you just crawled through the desert and came out with a mouth full of sand. You've got to quench that thirst in your body. So, quenching is a good thing, right?

Or wrong? I guess maybe it depends. It may be a good thing when you are thirsty for water, but God tells us in Thessalonians that in our relationship with him, the act of quenching is a bad thing. As a Christian and a firm believer that Christ wants to take an active role in his children's lives, I am reminded daily that quenching is bad—if what I am quenching is the very presence of Christ in my life—the one thing I'd give anything to feel more of.

Ironically, I actually wrote the notes for this devotion months before I finished it. Right in the middle of my frustration at my inability to complete this devotion, it dawned on me that God was allowing me to endure a gut-wrenching, Spirit-quenching dry spell. I guess he thought I would be better able to share with you firsthand the danger of suppressing the Spirit of God in our lives.

Here's what I figured out about myself. I personally tend to stifle Christ's Spirit in three main ways: I take on too much activity, I rely completely on my own abilities and become self-absorbed, or I get a negative attitude and slide right on into a period of depression.

From my teenage years to my adulthood, my life continues to follow this same Spirit-quenching pattern, over and over again! I was incapable of writing this devotion for a whole month because I got so bogged down by the very three things that I just mentioned! The same thing happened when I went to edit it. Feeling guilt-ridden that I still hadn't learned this lesson, I almost threw the pages on the floor just to avoid the issue.

I am a mover and a shaker. I love activity. I love to do things and make to-do lists just so I can scratch something off! It makes me feel so accomplished. But check out my recent list of activities: a full-time job, choreographing for drill team, doing a Bible study at home and in Houston, a dancing program at the ballet studio, performing at church, holding on to a dating relationship and writing this book!

Do you get my point? Were any of these activities bad? Absolutely not—at least not in and of themselves. But too much activity at one time will eventually consume us and drown out the fire we have for Christ. Busyness takes over our quality prayer time, our service to him and our ability to just sit quietly in his peace.

Due to my busy schedule, I started to rely too heavily on myself. What is on *my* calendar? Where do *I* have to be? Do *I* have everything I need? Did I finish the things on *my* list? How am *I* ever going to get all of this done? *I* am losing *my* mind! You see? A heart normally in love with serving Christ and loving others quickly became quenched by a pool of "me juice." My new short temper and self-absorption began to affect all of the people I love and care for.

Finally, my negative attitude and depression kicked into overdrive. As I failed to meet the demands of my busy schedule, I felt like a loser. I not only beat myself up for my failure to finish what I started, but I beat myself up over my looks, my talents, my abilities, my . . . you name it. Pretty soon I saw myself as an unattractive, untalented person that was useless to everyone. And for the most part, I was. Not useless in the way I saw it. I didn't look any different physically, but I had certainly changed on the inside. I had gotten an ugly attitude. I had not lost my abilities, except for my ability to serve. I

was temporarily out of service as a result of my screwed-up outlook.

I have to tell you—I was absolutely miserable. I stifled God's Spirit by crowding my heart and soul with self-pity and busyness. And when God's Spirit got quenched, my own started to wither away as well. I felt lost, lonely and disgusted. But that was my own choice; I didn't have to be that way, and it wasn't until I prayed about it, slowed down my activity and started focusing on Christ and others again that I began to feel better. The fire was back, burning once again, and my heart's spirit was unstifled, unquenched and full of joy!

What is it that douses your fire? Is it busyness? loneliness? Perhaps it's anger, jealousy, depression or maybe not enough activity! Whatever it is, don't be afraid to identify your "spirit-quencher" and be ready to fight it off when it starts to drown your heart! Although all kinds of drink companies promote their product's thirst-quenching ability, I'm sticking with my spiritual thirst as a reminder of my need for the Spirit's living water. A well-balanced life lived for Christ—now *that* does your body good!

Anything But Plastic

1. Read Galatians 5:16. What does this verse say happens when you don't live your life in the Holy Spirit?

2. List some of the activities that you have going on in your life right now.

   As I mentioned before, your activities may not be bad, but too many activities at one time may eventually get you! What could you eliminate from your life right now that might free up more time to be filled with the Holy Spirit?

3. Satan attacks you where he knows he can bring you down. Name one or several of your internal Spirit-quenchers.

4. Read Romans 8:26, 27. Is there a place in your life in which you could really use the Holy Spirit to groan on your behalf? What is it? Is there something you have a hard time praying for? What do these verses say that the Holy Spirit will do for you?

5. Read Psalm 51:10-13. At times, when I struggle with a Spirit-quenched life, these verses have been all I could pray. How do they make you feel?

Are you suffering a Spirit-quenched walk or are you thirsting every day for Jesus? What indicators in your life tell you what your thirst conditions are?

Beyond Plastic . . . .

I share this devotion with you from unpleasant experience, but I also speak out of a renewed spirit! Do not let your Spirit be stifled. We miss out on so much from God when we're drowning in "me-juice"!

TRUE COLORS

Thank you for making me so wonderfully complex!

Psalm 139:14

As kids, my sister and I used to rip the wrappers off crayons and then scrape a pair of scissors up and down the sides of the colors. Then we dropped our curlicues onto some waxed paper, smeared them around into a perfectly arranged pattern and ironed another sheet of paper on top to melt the shavings.

Once we finished, we would hang them up in the window or hold them up to the light. When you're eight years old, this is cool! My sister and I each had our very own hand-made kaleidoscope. What we never realized is that an activity that gave us such a cheap thrill is kind of like the priceless activity that continues to bring great joy to God, our creator. Guess what? God likes to play with colors too! You and me! We're his kaleidoscopic creations.

I wonder why it is, when we can see in Psalm 139 that we are so wonderfully complex, that so many of us struggle with our self-image. I've got to confess to you—once I hit my mid-teens, this became one of my main struggles in my walk with Christ. I am ashamed when I think of the number of days I have wasted being depressed and having negative thoughts about who I am. I'm talking about major crying sessions and pity parties: I often feel fat, unattractive, unsuccessful, unacceptable, un-anything. Certainly not special. Even when others try to encourage me, I still wallow in my poor self-image. But it shouldn't matter if others think I am pretty or smart or valuable. In the big scheme of things, what matters is that every time I bash myself—

every time I look in the mirror and see ugly—I cut down and rip apart one of God's creations, one of his kaleidoscopes.

One dictionary describes a *kaleidoscope* like this: 1) a tube-like instrument containing loose bits of colored glass and plastic reflected by mirrors so that various symmetrical patterns appear when the tube is rotated; 2) anything that is constantly changing, as in color and pattern.

I know—you're not a tube; but definition number two does describe us to a *t*! We are constantly changing. But what I think is really cool is the origin of the word *kaleidoscope*. In Greek, the prefix *kalos* means "beautiful." The suffix *eidos* means "form." Put together, a kaleidoscope is a "beautiful form"—a beautiful creation. You and I are beautiful creations—unique and most definitely constantly changing. There's no getting around what Psalm 139 says. God wove each of us together. He has a specific pattern or design for each of his kaleidoscopes. All of your wax shavings and curlicues are in order, with just the right mix of looks, humor, talents, humility, stubbornness, strengths and weaknesses.

When we look in a mirror and don't like what we see, we have to get over it. We have to remember that there is a way better mirror than the one hanging on our bathroom wall. This mirror is Christ. He reflects our true colors in a way the bathroom mirror can't do.

Think about it. Wax paper and color shavings wouldn't be so much fun if you held them up to the window at night. Without your source of light, you would be just like a kaleidoscope that has been laid down on a table or put in a dark drawer away from a window. You are not a functioning "beautiful form" if your life has grown too busy, if you've strayed from a Christlike lifestyle, or if you've just gotten relaxed in your walk with Christ.

We can only see our true beauty, our beautiful changing pattern, when light is reflected through us. If our focus is wrapped up in our own failures, we can't see Christ as our source of light. He's busy—has been since the day we were born—shining forth his radiance through us. Contrary to the way you feel, you are a kaleidoscope—a beautiful form. So, eyes off the mirror and into the light!

Anything But Plastic

1. Take a few moments to describe some of your colors. What makes you unique physically? emotionally? spiritually?

2. Are there times in your life when you lose confidence in who you are—times when you cut down or insult the very "beautiful form" God made you? Think about your life. When are you low? What gets you down? Describe some of those situations below.

3. Read John 1:9. How are your colors visible to others, as well as yourself? Who is the true light? Does God only choose to enlighten a few people?

4. Read Ephesians 5:8. Have your colors always been as visible to the outside world as they may be now? According to this passage, what were you before inviting Christ into your life?

Read 1 John 1:7. Where does this verse say that God can be found? Where should you strive to walk?

5. What colors of your kaleidoscope are getting a little dull and dingy, perhaps less brilliant? Stop and consider your "colors" and jot a little summary below.

Beyond Plastic . . . .

Not only are kaleidoscopes beautiful when held up to the light, but they are especially fascinating when they are twisted and turned by the spectator. When the colored patterns change and converge, you can truly see the beauty of the kaleidoscope.

God is the primary spectator in your life. Sometimes the twisting and turning may cause your picture to get fuzzy for a while. But if we let God fine-tune us, our lives will come brilliantly back into focus!

A RULE FOR LIFE

Since everything God created is good, we should not reject any of it. We may receive it gladly, with thankful hearts.

1 Timothy 4:4

My niece and nephew, respectively four and six years old at the time, once reminded me just how special God intended that ladies be treated. While the three of us were playing one day, my niece Jordan handed out toy ponies. She then assigned roles to each of us, playing the part of the mommy horse herself.

Joshua, my nephew, trotted his teenage boy horse up to mine and said, "Would you like to go on a date?"

My pony replied to his, "Sure! Where are we going?"

"To the school dance party," replied pony-boy.

"What time are you picking me up?" I whinnied.

"How about 6:30?" he said.

So our two ponies agreed to a first date, and the colt asked the filly out again, only this time he first pranced up to Mamma horse and out of his mouth came the words, "May I take your daughter on a date?"

Mamma horse replied, "Sure!"

The adults who were also in the room coaxed Mamma horse to set the rules for the date. Jordan thought for a moment and then laid down the rules. Forget the warnings about alcohol, parties, going out in a group, curfews, designated drivers or any other difficult dilemmas like the ones you face today. After much thought the most important thing that sprang to her mind was this: "There will be no running!"

It sounds silly, I know. After all, what does running have to do with teenagers and their dating lives, anyway? But do you know? My four-year-old niece had the right idea. Why shouldn't the rules be that easy?

Should you feel pressure to go on a date where you have to worry about the actions of a guy—the very guy to whose protection your parents entrusted you? If a guy makes you question your standards, consider doing things you know you should not do, feel like anything less than a lady or wonder if he has your safety or best interest at heart, then why should you settle for him? No matter how much you like him, if you have to question his character—why bother?

Some girls feel like they always have to have a boyfriend. These girls seem to be so uncomfortable and unsure about themselves when they don't have boyfriends. Sometimes you can see females quietly change who they really are, in order to please some guy. At times, the easy way out seems to be to act like someone other than yourself. There is fear in being who you really are, because if you are the genuine "you," maybe the guy won't like you. Everyone wants to be liked.

I haven't dated a whole lot in my life. Now in my early thirties, I can actually count the number of guys I've dated on one hand! This lack of experience is good and bad. On the plus side, I get hurt less! But I also have to learn a lot each time I date someone new. But while I am without a guy, I discover more of my identity in God and the things I like about myself that make me who I am.

I know loneliness sometimes clouds our hearts and minds. But you and I are special to God, and he has great plans for each one of us, which may include someone to love! Then again, I have no doubt that God has more for you to do in this life than just finding your perfect love match. In any case, don't settle for someone who doesn't deserve you and hasn't earned the right to love you. I still pray almost daily that God will keep me from just settling for anyone and help me await his plans for me!

And if you do receive the blessing of that man you may have been praying for and dreaming of, just remember the rule: "There will be no running!"

. . . .

1. Have your parents set any boundaries for you regarding your dating life or your interaction with boys? What are those boundaries?

Have you personally set any rules for yourself regarding your behavior? If you have some thoughts, list them below.

If you haven't set guidelines, maybe now is a good time to do so. You could pray that God would help you set standards for yourself before it's too late to rethink your actions.

2. Read Genesis 1:27. How does this verse make you feel about God's feelings toward you?

Read 1 Timothy 4:4. Who or what is good, according to this verse?

Read Psalm 139:13, 14. What is the word this psalm uses to describe God's works?

3. In this book, you've read a lot about weaknesses and the things you may need to work on. Let's take a second to brag about God. Name three or four attributes, characteristics or talents you possess (all of which come from God) that you are proud of!

4. Why do you think some girls feel like they need a boyfriend at all times?

Read 2 Corinthians 3:5; 9:8. Who does the provision for all that you need come from?

Beyond Plastic . . . .

Keep the rules simple. Be who you really are and allow God to be your guide in all of your relationships, whether romantic or not.

NEED A PEDICURE?

How beautiful are the feet of those who bring good news!

Romans 10:15

Come on—was Paul really serious when he wrote this? When you get down to it, how beautiful *are* feet? Had Paul seen mine, he might have rewritten this verse in Romans. I have what you call "dancer's feet." They are *not* looking too hot after years of sheer torture—dancing barefoot and cramming them into pointe shoes.

My beloved feet are decorated with scars, spots, calluses, abrasions and protruding bunions. I pop my toes constantly while I'm dancing in order to keep my feet limber. Come to think of it, I pop them even when I'm not dancing. I have one toe that cracks no matter what, so I snap that one just to annoy my mom! To top it off, one of my wild habits is the way I treat my feet; I wear a gold toe ring and habitually paint my toenails with bright,

obnoxious colors in order to hide all of the scratches and discolorations. Today's hue of choice happens to be a bright powder blue. So, I'm really rethinking this how–beautiful-are-the-feet thing.

Then again, Paul never said anything about clean feet, or unscarred, unscratched appendages. In Romans 10, he speaks about the *purpose* of the feet. Think about it for a second. What is the purpose of your feet, other than to hold you up and get you from here to there?

Although mine are not particularly attractive, I've learned to praise God for what he lets me do because of my feet. I figure that I actually serve him with my feet. As a dancer in high school, God allowed me to love and set an example for those around me on the dance team. He's taken these same efforts into my career. Because of my feet and my use of them as a dance teacher and drill team director, I believe God uses me as a role model, encourager and mentor for the many teenagers I work with. He's also allowed me to praise him through praise-and-worship dancing at church.

In the non-dancing realm, God leads me to many places and situations in order to do his work—perhaps to pray for someone, to uplift and encourage someone, or to be the peacemaker in a situation—you know, to bring the good news of Christ. Just this morning on my way to the drive-thru, I saw a hitchhiker on the road. Because of my soda craving, a stranger was lifted to the Father in prayer!

I have always liked my feet and find them kind of pretty, in an ugly sort of way! As a matter of fact, I think I like them even more the uglier they get and the more miles I've put on them. I pamper my feet with fun shoes, fragrant sprays and foot lotion. After all, they are my messengers, so I must keep them oiled and ready to go!

What good news do your feet bring? What stories can your feet tell? Perhaps they carry you to places of ministry? Maybe your trip to school becomes your mission field? Of course I'm talking about physical feet—but I mean your spiritual feet too! Are they ready? You never know when they may be called to duty. God likes those ugly worn-in hooves—feet that serve God are hot stuff!

Anything But Plastic

. . . .

1. What do you think of your feet? Can you look at your feet and remember any particular thing that has happened to cause them to look the way they do?

   On a more spiritual level, can you remember some times when your feet have been your messengers, when you were actively serving God in a situation?

2. Think for a moment about the feet of Christ. What must Jesus' feet have looked like? Although Jesus was reverent and still when his Father called him to be, he also put lots of miles on those feet, walking many roads and touching many people because of his willingness to go where God called him.

   Spend a few minutes reading the following Scriptures: Matthew 28:8, 9; Mark 5:22; Luke 7:36–46; Luke 24:39. There are many references to Jesus' feet in Scripture. Why do you think people fell at his feet and worshiped there?

3. What should the dirt on Jesus' feet mean to us? What kind of adjectives would you use to describe the results of Jesus' ministry?

Read Luke 24:39. Why did Jesus tell the two disciples to look at his feet?

4. Read John 13:1-10. What do you find strange about this event? Do you think Jesus should have been pampering others' feet? Why or why not?

What do you think this act of washing feet symbolizes?

5. Are your feet a little too clean? Have you been so consumed with your own life that you've neglected to go into service to others? Where do you think God may be calling you to use your feet to deliver good news?

Beyond Plastic

Pray that God will show you how he wants to use you on a daily basis to be his messenger. Paint those toes and lather on the lotion. Your feet are going to be awfully busy!

CATCH ME, DADDY!

Trust is a tricky thing. In one breath your parents may tell you that they don't trust you to go somewhere alone, but in the next breath they tell you that you need to trust them. Don't trust a stranger, but trust an emergency paramedic you've never seen before to take care of you. Don't trust things that look too good to be true, but trust God even though you can't see him at all. See what I mean? It's tricky.

There are days when we ask ourselves, *Is there anyone I can trust? Anyone who feels the same way I do? Is there someone who sees my hurt but won't make fun of me for it? Anyone I can latch onto and depend on, without having to explain the way I feel? Anyone who will listen to me without betraying my thoughts to others?* Sadly, during many of those times when we are afraid to trust,

we may simply feel alone and choose not to trust at all.

Why don't we trust people? Do we fear that people don't understand where we are coming from? That they just can't relate? Maybe we have a fear of being made fun of or we fear betrayal. We tell someone something in the strictest confidence and they spill it to someone else. Or maybe if we choose to trust someone else, we become vulnerable and reveal our raw, inner thoughts and feelings. Whatever the reason, it is hard to trust!

It used to be so much easier to do when we were younger. I often think it would be great to be a little girl again. I don't ever remember being worried as a kid! My parents never left me anywhere. They took me to the doctor when I was sick. They fed me. They tucked me in at night. I never had to worry about the alligators at the foot of the bed, because someone always checked first before I crawled in.

What about swimming at the pool? Who needed floaties? When I ran to the edge of the pool and yelled, "Catch me, Daddy!" there was never a doubt in my mind that Dad's open arms wouldn't be on the other end of that jump! Mom or Dad always waited in the pool to put me safely back up on the edge so I could do it again and again. *Catch me!* Jump, feel the breeze on my face, the water on my back and the strong arms propelling me back to the poolside. There was a safe thrill to the whole routine! Oh, to be a kid again!

But how quickly I got too brave. Without realizing it, I swam right away from the safe arms of my dad. Soon, I was paddling around with my eyes shut, playing Marco Polo. After that, I ventured out of the shallow end completely. I was now with the big kids playing Shark in the deep end, fearlessly swimming down 9 feet to touch the drain on the bottom before "Jaws" got me. But even without the floaties on, there was always a lifeguard on duty. Trust was easy with the high school hottie perched on the guard tower, ready to jump in and save me at a moment's notice.

I guess I never realized that circumstances could have broken my trust so easily. I never considered that I could have gotten my hair caught in the deep-end drain. I never dreamed that the guy on duty was busy scamming on the high school babe in the bikini—not really keeping a watchful eye on me at all. When I look back on it now, swimming was kind of dangerous.

Now as an adult, I think it's still a little risky. Even though floating around in the pool makes for a fun afternoon, in the back of my head I know the sun is always ready to harm my fair skin with its cancer-causing UV rays. I've still got hair—and there's still a drain! And I don't ever live down the danger of wearing my bathing suit to the public pool, outside the safety of my own backyard. There is no way to trust that people won't stare at me and think, *When did the beached whale float in?*

Was it wrong for me to be so free-spirited and trusting as a kid? What was I thinking? Or maybe there is something wrong with me now! Am I ready and willing to dive into life—sharks or not—when I know that God is the lifeguard on duty? He is perched up high with a watchful eye on his children as we swim through this life. Can I shut my eyes and lie back and float into the very obvious circumstances that he is providing? Do

I trust him to guide me? Am I brave or patient enough to cry out, "Marco!" and wait in faith and trust for him to answer, "Polo!" in his own perfect timing?

How sad is it that we refuse to trust God at times, even though he meets all of the right criteria to deserve our trust? He loves us *more* than we deserve! He knows us far better than we know ourselves! And he's the best replacement for anything or anyone that we could choose to trust. We can move out of the shallow end into the deep areas of our fears and worries and just tell him where it hurts. There's no need for sunscreen. He won't expose us to more than we can handle. He will keep us safe from dangerous elements in our lives when we just lean on him. It should be so reaffirming to know that when we feel like we can't trust anyone around us, we still can trust in God!

Innocent trust and a little child-like faith would do us all some good. In our hearts, we can be just like that free-spirited child again. We can choose to trust him implicitly—no questions asked! So fling off your floaties of fear and take a flying leap into the life God has planned for you. Just yell, "Catch me, Daddy!" and jump. God's got you covered!

Anything But Plastic

1. There are several ways you trust in God. Initially, you must trust in him with your heart and commit your life to him as a Christian. Have you committed your heart to God? Do you know him personally? If not, now is the perfect time to trust God and place your life in his hands.

   The second way we trust God is with the daily details of our lives, a task that is often easier said than done. Read the following verses and answer the questions.

   Psalm 25:2. In whom does David choose to trust?

   Psalm 31:6. How about in this verse? Who does David proclaim that he trusts?

   Psalm 20:7. What does David trust here?

2. It is often easy to trust in people and things, because they are tangible. List below three things or people in which you trust and the reasons why you trust them.

3. Let's take that trust to a higher level: trusting in things you *can't* see. Think of all of the people in the Bible who did huge tasks for God without being able to see him at all! That's what I call ultimate trust! Read Genesis 6:13–22; 7:1–5. What did Noah do? Do you think it was easy for him to do this task with only God's prompting? Why or why not?

If God asked you to do in your generation what Noah did in his, what do you think your peers would say about you? Would you care what they thought? Do you think you would have the courage to do something that seemed so absurd to everyone else around you? Why or why not?

Read Exodus 3:6-12. What did God call Moses to do? It took years for Moses to take these people on a journey that should have taken weeks. Why do you think that God possibly allowed his peoples' journey to take so long?

4. When things get crazy in your life, what shakes your ability to trust? Name some specific circumstances and things that test you. Be honest.

5. Read Proverbs 3:5, 6. How should you trust in God? What should you not depend on? With how much of your life should you trust him? What will happen if you do trust in him?

Beyond Plastic . . . .

Trusting is a daily thing. It doesn't just happen. You must choose to keep your heart committed to God in trust, despite the bad times, fights, divorces, break-ups, misunderstandings, etc. Take a few minutes to ask God to help you trust in him. He is waiting to catch you and he wants to direct you and keep you in his plans!

DOWN IN THE VALLEY

I wrote this devotion after what I can honestly say was one of the worst weeks of my life. I will attempt to spare you too many boring details, but it all started with Christmas break—you know, the time of the year that should be relaxing and full of good times? Well, before I knew it, I was shopping for "her" and cooking for "them." I danced in the Nutcracker, wrapped presents, cleaned house and practiced for a Christmas Eve performance at church. I fixed costumes, visited some people in one town, drove to see some others in the next town and then returned to my town. Throw in Christmas Day, a sick boyfriend, my birthday and the next thing I knew, I was spread so thinly that I became a nervous wreck; I was exhausted and slipped into a state of mild depression,

at which point I cried and stressed out for over a week.

During those weeks that followed, Satan saw my busyness as a prime opportunity to sneak up and attack me. All it took was for me to occupy myself doing good things. As I stayed busy, I allowed my prayer and Bible study time to take the back burner, while Satan celebrated in my stress and pain. Jeremiah 1:19 reminds me that Satan definitely means all of his pranks for evil. For a week, he won battles in my life. I prayed and searched Scripture to pull me out of my depression, but Satan kept fighting to keep me in that state of mind. And then one morning it happened. I prayed on my way to work that the Lord would speak to me and get my attention in *any* way that he saw fit. I should have known that if I genuinely prayed for a wake-up call, God would sincerely deal with me. He answered my prayer, bringing me humbly to my knees in order to snap me out of my mood.

His method was to speak to me through a fifteen-year-old student of mine. In my depressed and selfish state, I did one of the things that I hate more than anything in the world—I hurt someone's feelings. I said things unintentionally and lashed out with comments that I immediately regretted, things that made me feel worse for saying them and worse still for harming this young girl whom it was my responsibility to mentor. As she wiped tears from her eyes and as I apologized to her, it hit me. I had allowed Satan to twist my attitude, joyfulness and sensitivity to others to the point where I would use my pain to cause someone else to feel just as miserable as I did. God held me accountable to my prayer by sending this young friend my way that day. He taught me a lesson through tough love.

I am thankful that God is a God of second chances—that instead of allowing evil to overcome me, he delivered me and set my feet on firm ground once again. He promises in his Word to keep us from being overcome. His presence was with me, whether I recognized it or not, during my whole time of stress. In my desperate cry for help from the bottom of the valley, he humbled me and reminded me that only when my focus is right will I not be overcome. Satan meant all of it for evil, but I am blessed that God meant those weeks, in the long run, for good.

Anything But Plastic

· ·

1. Have you ever gone through a circumstance or series of events that sent you on a downward spiral regarding your attitude? Describe the situation.

What did you think about yourself and your attitude once you overcame the emotions?

2. Can you pick out a time in your life when you reacted to stress with a Christ-filled spirit? How did it differ from your more depressed or negative reaction?

Read Proverbs 15:13. What happens when the heart is sad? What is the result of a glad heart?

Read Ecclesiastes 11:10. What does Scripture say we should do with grief or pain? How do you think God feels when you come to him in your sadness and despair and cry out to him, rather than wallowing in self-pity?

3. On the other hand what do you think it does to God's heart when you hurt someone with your words?

Read Proverbs 10:10, 11. What do people who wink at wrong do? What do evil people do?

Even though you may not think of yourself as a wicked person, you are not doing God's will when you hurt others. Can you describe a time you hurt someone with your words? What happened?

How did it make you feel to hurt someone else? Did you try to fix the situation? How?

4. Read Matthew 6:14, 15; Mark 11:26. What do these verses say happens when you don't forgive others? How do you do at showing mercy?

Beyond Plastic . . . .

There is good news, despite all the sorrow and frustration that comes our way. Isaiah 51:11 says "Sorrow and mourning will disappear, and they will be overcome with joy and gladness." Satan wants to keep us stuck in depression, but God has other plans!

TAKE THAT!

Have you ever suffered a major disappointment in your life at the hands of someone else? Maybe you were waiting on friends to follow through on a commitment, and they left you hanging. Or you were waiting patiently to be accepted into a club and found out they didn't want you. Or you were working on a group project, only to find yourself doing all of the work while your other group members put their names on the project and took credit for it. Perhaps you were striving for an accomplishment in a sport, art or academics and someone else did something that got in your way.

I have suffered through these incidents and then some. I had an acquaintance back in my carless years who used to promise to give me rides. When I went outside to wait for her, I would find myself standing on my driveway for many minutes after her proclaimed pick-up time, knowing deep down that she would never show up. I have had other friends who talked big, but when it was time to deliver, they had long since forgotten any of the promises they had made. These disappointments seem minor in the grand scheme of things, but when someone hurts your feelings undeservingly, it definitely impacts you.

What is important is how we react to these situations. It is so easy to want to spite the people that hurt us to let them know how we really feel—to make a promise to them and then purposely break it just to get back at them. Does the expression, "In your face!" sound familiar to you? When people hurt us, our human reaction is to stand up for ourselves with an in-your-face kind of attitude.

The events of 9/11 have made many people in our country angry, and their natural reaction is to fight back with a vengeance against those who invaded our peace and security and killed many of our citizens. We all have personal situations where the desire to act with vengeance might run fervently through our veins.

My worst memory of this vengeful attitude goes back about six years. I once applied for a job that I was well qualified for. After a long, strenuous interview process, however, I didn't get the job. I know now that God had different plans for me. It wasn't so much the disappointment of not getting the job that infuriated me, but more the unprofessional way in which I found out about the interview results. I discovered my rejection by word of mouth from people in the community and my own students, who knew before I did. It was not until three days after I first heard, that I even received a professional letter of rejection. It angered me to think of the way the situation was handled, and it took me some time to forgive the people who allowed it to happen.

I am grateful, however, that God is the God of vengeance. Many verses in his Word remind us that he is the peacemaker. He is also our avenger. It is not our job to fight back against people that hurt us, no matter how much we may want to do so. I know that no scheme I could ever come up with would actually fix any situation. I am certain that if I fought back, it would only make things worse. When we react out of bitterness, jealousy or anger, we are not capable of reflecting Christ's attitude or any amount of level-headedness.

What about you? Has someone hurt you lately? Do you have a friend, teacher or employer who seems to go to any measure to see to it that you are miserable? Is someone competing with you? trying to keep you from being successful? Do you know someone that will hurt others in an effort to keep another person from being happy, or just to get what he or she wants?

You can celebrate the fact that God is not through with the situation. We can wait patiently for him. The last word will be his, and you can rest assured that he will favor you in your faithfulness. He will not allow people who scheme against his children to succeed in the end. God tells us not to worry, for vengeance is his.

Anything But Plastic

. . . .

1. Can you think of a situation in your life when someone really hurt you? If you can't think of an incident in your own life, what about one that happened to a friend or a family member? Briefly explain. What was your reaction or the other person's reaction toward the person who caused pain?

2. Look up the word *vengeance* in the dictionary and define it below.

   Read Deuteronomy 32:35. Why do you think it is important to leave the act of vengeance to God?

   Have you ever been angry at someone and decided to take matters into your own hands? What did you do? What happened as a result of your reaction? How did you feel when you were done playing the avenger?

3. Read Deuteronomy 32:35 again, and add verse 36 to it. Why do you think God's timing is better than ours when it comes to getting back at someone?

4. Read 2 Samuel 22:20-27. David wrote this after years of running from his enemy Saul. All in all, I'd say David did a good job of leaving the treatment of Saul in God's hands. Why did God rescue and reward David? What do you learn about the way David treated Saul?

If you were to study the history of Saul and David, you would see that David had every right to be angry at Saul. Saul chased David, was out to kill him, betrayed him and tried to take David's best friend away from him. Is your reaction to your enemies as honorable and pure as David's was to Saul? Consider your personal actions and give an honest and brief summary below.

5. Read Psalm 37:7. God wants you to give him your thoughts regarding those who do evil to you. When you do, he gives you three commands. What are they?

Beyond Plastic

All this is easier said than done, I know. But God's Word says plainly, loudly and clearly: getting back at people is not your job. If you quietly sit back and pray for your attitude, God will take care of the rest. Start praying now for future situations—that you would react to your enemy with the purity and blamelessness of David.

WALK ON

Observe the requirements of the Lord your God and follow all his ways. Keep each of the laws, commands, regulations, and stipulations written in the law of Moses so that you will be successful in all you do and wherever you go.

1 Kings 2:3

You would think that the act of walking would be a very simple thing, wouldn't you? You've been walking since you were a toddler. You endured your share of falls and scraped knees. I mean, how hard can it be to put one foot in front of the other? However, how many times do you walk next to someone who outstrides you? They leave you choking in their dust yelling, "Slow down!" or "Wait up!" Maybe *you* are the one that nobody can keep up with. That happens to be me. I'm one of those people who is all limbs—especially legs— and I can take off with the best of them!

In the drill team world, there are some basic rules we have always followed for walking—yes, we even have rules for walking. Your step size or stride must be something that everyone can keep up

with. Sometimes taller people have to take smaller steps than what are natural for them so that the shorter ones can keep up; and there are times when the little ones just have to leap in order to accommodate the tall people.

It's the same in our relationship with God. I imagine he sometimes gets very bored walking at our stubbornly slow pace; yet there are times we feel as if he is opening the gap between his steps and ours so that we can barely keep up. Despite how it appears, he never makes us leap farther than we can manage.

Also, the speed of the walk is an important factor to consider. The pace that we keep must be consistent enough that everyone can walk comfortably. Either too fast or too slow, and the steps become uncomfortable for the walkers. If the steps are too fast, there is a sense of panic in the movement. If the walking is too slow, the pace becomes monotonous and the movement begins to look as if we are headed to a funeral. In our walk with him, God knows exactly at which tempo to set our walk, even if we tend to disagree with his timing.

Most importantly, when we walk, we should always "guide"—which in drill team world is code for "Watch where you're going." In order to keep multiple people in line, we take every step while sharing a common focus. Our focus generally goes to the tallest member, who maintains her position in the center of the line. She is the one who can see out and beyond everyone and is able to capture the big picture of where the walk is taking the group. If the medium-height girls look to the tall ones and the short ones look to the medium ones, then everyone arrives at the same destination, at the same time, and without injury.

This same rule is true of our walk with Christ. He serves as our leader, or the center, of our walk. We are required to guide to him. Even if we can't see him exactly with our eyes because someone or something blocks our view, we have to remember two things: he can see the big picture and he knows exactly where he is leading us.

Contrary to what we feel as walkers, God never moves too quickly or too slowly; his steps are never too big or too small; his path is neither too planned nor too unpredictable. He knows every straight way, every unexpected curve and every bump in the road. Because we know that God promises to guide us, we should be able to move comfortably and faithfully through our walk with him. Guide to God and allow him to help you walk in his ways.

Anything But Plastic

. . . .

1. The physical act of walking sounds quite easy, I know! But remember, you didn't come out of the womb doing it! In what ways do you feel like you've made progress from crawling to walking in your relationship with Christ?

2. Read Isaiah 40:31. Even though you may struggle with the step size God asks you to take in your life, what does this verse promise you about your energy level if you walk with and wait in him?

   Read Psalm 23:3. Not only will God restore your energy, but how else will he spiritually give you rest?

3. Read Leviticus 26:3, 4. God commands his children to walk in his commandments. However, when did he promise to give rains and fruit-bearing evidence? Are our seasons and God's seasons the same?

4. What are some things in the world that you sometimes focus on for help when you get tired of walking? Do you eat when you are sad? Shop when you get stressed out? When and how does your focus move off of your walk with Christ and onto other things?

Read 2 Corinthians 5:7. How are you to live? What does this mean to you?

5. Read Hebrews 12:2. Where should you keep your eyes? What will God do with your faith as a result of your focus on him?

Who has God placed higher up in your spiritual "height line" to help you? List several people you look to for spiritual guidance and a specific way they nurture you in your walk.

Is there someone you feel that God wants *you* to help guide on their journey in Christ?

Beyond Plastic . . . .

Remember, the walk is a great adventure, and God will take care of the details. Keep your eyes on the one who can see the whole route; relax and take in the scenic view. The journey is as God chooses; you might as well enjoy it!

COUNT ON IT

Well, I've been waiting for the magic potion—the exactly right thing to write about, that perfect way to finish off this book. I've thought and racked my brain and mulled it over until I realized the perfect thing to write about is the fact that this is the last devotion. The big number Fifty-One. The end all and be all. The last hurrah. The whole shebang. Well, you get the point.

So what's the big deal with number fifty-one? Nothing. It's just a number. But it's a big deal for me because it's the end of this book I've been carrying around for the last five or six years.

Numbers don't mean much of anything by themselves, but they can become very important. What did you get on your last test? Was it 100 percent or 40 percent?

What's the number of weeks your friend wouldn't speak to you? How many days has someone you love been sick? How much money do you need to go to college? What's the number of times someone has hurt your feelings or the number of fights your parents have had lately? You see, numbers can be very important.

I think God likes numbers. Just look at some of the examples he put in his Word. The list is super-long even if we only looked in the Old Testament at the number of "thou shalts" and "thou shalt nots" listed for the people of Israel. But let's just look at some of the extremely significant numbers in the indisputable Word of God.

God created the heavens and the earth in seven days.

Jesus had a tight group of friends—twelve disciples.

He had an even closer inner circle of three friends. And while we're on the number three, how about the fact that Jesus rose again on the third day? That's significant!

Then there's the fact that Jesus, with God the Father and the Holy Spirit, makes up the Trinity—yet another significant three!

And how about the Ten Commandments—not eight, not fifteen, but precisely ten?

There were twelve tribes of Israel.

Noah's ark floated for forty days and forty nights.

Israel wandered in the desert for forty years.

We are supposed to forgive our brothers seven times seventy times.

That's a lot of numbers, and we are just scraping the tip of the iceberg. What makes me feel good is that we are even told that God knows the number of tears we cry, the number of our thoughts and the number of hairs on our heads. I find that last detail extremely comical since I shed like a cat and feel like I am going bald half of the time. I can just imagine God saying, "Mieka's hair count: 2,456. Oh no, there goes another one. 2,455. No, wait. 2,454. Uh, oh. I think three fell out. So that would be 2,451. Ugh! She just pulled out three gray ones at the sink. Why did I ever tell my children I would keep count of those stupid hairs anyway?"

God's not the only numbers fan. I'm into numbers as well. I'll let you in on one of the obnoxious little things that my dad and I do. As Christians, we know that nothing's ever better than the intimate time we spend in prayer with God. Nothing can calm us like carrying our worries to Christ and having him lift those burdens. Nothing makes us feel purer than confessing our sins and allowing God to wash us clean. My family knows that prayer is our lifeline. But sometimes when we get impatient or frustrated, we have a little prayer game that we play—and it is all based on numbers.

Even though I know that there is power in prayer, there are times in the smallness of my mind that I feel like giving up. I mean, what about the never-ending, month to month, year after year, ongoing requests that we have in our lives? I often get tired of praying repeatedly for the same things. Do you ever feel like your prayers all sound the same? Over and over again you cry out—sounding like a whiner or a nagging kid. But you know if the request is important to you, it's important to God. So what is your reaction to the deafening silence?

In our family, we have a fast-food method of prayer. We've jokingly numbered all of our prayer requests. *God, I'm so tired tonight. Can I just lift up number twenty-two to you—you know, the guy thing? And a number thirteen, since my sister still isn't feeling well. Number eight is still hacking me off. I really just want something good to happen for my parents. Oh, and God? Number two again. Please forgive me for being jealous of the girl that just got a date with the guy I like!*

You and I both know that God is in the business of refining our character. I often wonder if God, to shape us and test our faithfulness, doesn't open up his book of trials and say, "Let's see. Mieka has been working on her struggle with bitterness. Let's send her trial number seventeen and see if she can withstand the pressure. Throw in a number six. We'll let her friend have another date to see if she will be happy just hanging with me. And just for the fun of it, maybe a number twelve? Will she keep her mouth shut when she gets upset so she won't fly off the handle and say something she'll regret?"

Please don't take this the wrong way. I am only joking. My family and I do kid around about this and we do number things. But when we actually pray, we don't really lift our pray requests like a value combo meal order. And God doesn't have a book of trials—he's not playing cruel number games with us.

Although I have had so many experiences to share with you through this book, don't think I'm preaching at you from some higher plane. I am still waiting—sometimes eagerly and sometimes impatiently—to get it together in my own life. I'm still not a complete original in this plastic world. But there are two things I have learned about prayer: my timing (usually on an I-want-it-now schedule) may not match up with God's, and my attitude while I wait for his answers should glorify God.

After all, if a prayer request is going to get the most awesome answer that exists, it has to come in God's timing and I'd better learn to wait for it with a smile and a sense of humor! We worship a God who tells us in 2 Thessalonians to "Pray without ceasing." God can count a never-ending list of prayers! So, whether you're counting sand, stars, hairs or tears, tally up! And let's hope God will find us faithful as he turns each one of us into an original creation!

Anything But Plastic

1. What do you think about numbers? Are you one of those that doesn't like the number thirteen? Do you ever follow the philosophy that the third time's a charm? What numbers are significant to you and why?

2. Read Matthew 10:29-31. How does God view you? How does this make you feel?

3. Are there some prayers that you feel like you want to number in your life? What are those ongoing requests?

4. What have you learned in praying for those things over a long period of time? What has God taught you about himself? What has God taught you about yourself?

5. What have you learned about God's characteristics as you have studied his Word and worked through this book? Do you think that God has a sense of humor? If so, what has happened in your life where you feel like you and God got a laugh out of the outcome?

Beyond Plastic . . . .

As you end this journey to become an original girl in a plastic world, think back on your progress. As you continue in your Christian walk, what plastic parts of your life do you think you might struggle with that you want to commit to God? He will continue to shape you into his original creation. All you have to do is ask! What areas of your life do you need to commit to him right now?

[Guys.]

What's floating around in their heads?
What makes them tick?
What makes them like you?

Secrets about Guys
[that shouldn't be secret]

Grace Dove

ISBN: 0-7847-1544-0

**Real stories. Practical tips. Biblical advice.
Reveals secrets about guys that girls want to know!**

This book helps girls understand why guys think the way they do,
how that affects girls, and how girls can relate to guys in a way that
pleases God.

Visit your local Christian bookstore
or www.standardpub.com
or call 1-800-543-1353.

ref·uge \ 're-fyüj \
shelter or protection from danger or distress

"My salvation and my honor come from God alone.
He is my refuge, a rock where no enemy can reach me.
O my people, trust in him at all times.
Pour out your heart to him,
for God is our refuge."
—*Psalm 62: 7, 8, NLT*

In the Old Testament God provided six "cities of refuge" where a person could seek safe haven from vengeance. These cities were places of protection. Today refuge™ will provide you the safe haven you need to grow in your relationship with God.

rfg www.rfgbooks.com